T0305734

ETHICS AND PROJECT MANAGEMENT

ETHICS AND PROJECT MANAGEMENT

RALPH L. KLIEM, PMP

CRC Press
Taylor & Francis Group
Boca Raton London New York

CRC Press is an imprint of the
Taylor & Francis Group, an **informa** business
AN AUERBACH BOOK

CRC Press
Taylor & Francis Group
6000 Broken Sound Parkway NW, Suite 300
Boca Raton, FL 33487-2742

Version Date: 20110504

International Standard Book Number: 978-1-4398-5261-3 (Hardback)

Library of Congress Cataloging-in-Publication Data

Kliem, Ralph L.
    Ethics and project management / Ralph L. Kliem.
      p. cm.
    Includes bibliographical references and index.
    ISBN 978-1-4398-5261-3
    1. Project management--Moral and ethical aspects. 2. Business ethics. 3. Professional ethics. I. Title.

HD69.P75K5784 2012
174'.4--dc23   2011017484

Visit the Taylor & Francis Web site at
http://www.taylorandfrancis.com

and the CRC Press Web site at
http://www.crcpress.com

To my great, honest friend, Howard McAuley

Contents

Preface xv
About the Author xix

Chapter 1   Ethics and Project Management 1

    1.1   What Is Ethics? 1
    1.2   Misperceptions about Ethics 3
        1.2.1   Ethics Has No Bottom-Line Value 3
        1.2.2   Ethics Is an Abstract, Not a Real, Concept 4
        1.2.3   Ethics Is a Stand-Alone Topic 4
        1.2.4   Ethics Is Applicable to People Only
                 at the Top of an Organization 4
        1.2.5   Ethics Applies to the Other Person 5
        1.2.6   Ethics Involves Only Compliance 5
        1.2.7   Ethics Deals Only with Matters That Are
                 "Black and White" in Nature 6
    1.3   Key Factors 6
        1.3.1   Peers 6
        1.3.2   Culture 7
        1.3.3   Power 7
        1.3.4   Competition 8
        1.3.5   Rewards 8
        1.3.6   Experiences 9
        1.3.7   Role Expectations 9
        1.3.8   Structure 10
        1.3.9   Management Style 10
    1.4   Common Terminology 10
        1.4.1   Values 11
        1.4.2   Trust 12
        1.4.3   Honesty 12
        1.4.4   Morality 12
        1.4.5   Character 13
        1.4.6   Virtue 14
        1.4.7   Fairness 14
        1.4.8   Integrity 15

1.5	Theoretical Underpinnings	15
1.6	Final Thoughts	17
1.7	Getting Started Checklist	18

Chapter 2   Why Ethics Should Matter to Project Managers............ 21

2.1	Unique Circumstances	21
2.2	Hard and Soft Ethical Issues	24
2.3	Consequences of Ethical Failure	31
2.4	Cloudy Perspective	32
2.5	The Ethical Dilemma	33
2.6	Two Key Considerations	35
2.7	Sensitivity of Issue	39
2.8	Intensity of Response	40
2.9	Final Thoughts	41
2.10	Getting Started Checklist	42

Chapter 3   Project Management Code of Ethics............ 47

3.1	Benefits	47
3.2	Downsides	49
3.3	Categories of Principles	49
	3.3.1	Character	51
	3.3.2	Career	51
	3.3.3	Competency	52
	3.3.4	Caretaking	54
	3.3.5	Confidentiality	56
	3.3.6	Communication	57
	3.3.7	Caring	58
	3.3.8	Conduct	61
	3.3.9	Commitment	62
	3.3.10	Compliance	63
3.4	Final Thoughts	64
3.5	Getting Started Checklist	64

Chapter 4   The Ethical Trends and Challenges Confronting Project Managers............ 69

| 4.1 | Global Trends | 69 |
| 4.2 | Adapting to Global Trends | 71 |

4.3   Straying from the High Road..........................74
       4.3.1   Organizational Perversities or Dysfunctions...74
       4.3.2   Tone at the Top........................75
       4.3.3   Pressure to Report Only Positive Data...........76
       4.3.4   Faster Results........................77
       4.3.5   No Trade-Offs between Efficiency and
               Effectiveness......................78
       4.3.6   Transglobal Operations.................79
       4.3.7   Diffusion of Accountability and Authority... 80
       4.3.8   Obedience to Authority................81
       4.3.9   Overemphasis on Legal Compliance............82
       4.3.10 Conflicting Laws and Regulations.................83
       4.3.11 Conflict of Interest and Conflicting
               Interest.........................84
       4.3.12 Pressure to Adjust Results to Meet
               Expectations......................85
       4.3.13 Restricted Access to Information.................86
       4.3.14 Reduced Cycle Time....................87
       4.3.15 Increased Customer Satisfaction.................88
       4.3.16 Stress on Becoming a Team Player................89
       4.3.17 Play by the Book.....................91
       4.3.18 Treat Symptoms as Fact..................91
       4.3.19 Reliance on Numbers...................93
       4.3.20 Desire for Agreement..................94
       4.3.21 Maintain Positive Working Relationships
               with Vendors, Partners, and Other
               External Stakeholders.................95
       4.3.22 Protecting One's Status and Position............ 96
4.4   Final Thoughts..........................97
4.5   Getting Started Checklist.......................98

Chapter 5   How Ethics Permeates the Entire Project Life Cycle... 101
5.1   Contextual Factors.........................101
5.2   Five Major Project Management Processes..............103
5.3   Categories of Ethical Dilemmas.....................104
       5.3.1   Compliance........................104
       5.3.2   Effectiveness.......................105
       5.3.3   Accurate and Timely Information................105

5.3.4 Efficiency..106
5.3.5 Protection of Resources...............................106
5.4 Ethics and Project Management Processes..............106
5.4.1 Initiating and Ethics...................................107
5.4.2 Low-Balling...107
5.4.3 Omitting Key Stakeholders..........................108
5.4.4 Misaligning with Organizational Goals 108
5.4.5 Conflicting Interest.....................................109
5.4.6 Not Clarifying Expectations........................109
5.4.7 Lying to Win Contract................................110
5.4.8 Sabotaging Relationships with Certain
      Stakeholders..110
5.4.9 Not Engaging in Good Faith Negotiations....111
5.5 Planning and Ethics...111
5.5.1 Padding..111
5.5.2 No Accountability......................................113
5.5.3 Lying...113
5.6 Executing and Ethics...114
5.6.1 Mischarging...114
5.6.2 Misinformation or Disinformation..............114
5.6.3 Straying from the Plan without
      Authorization......................................116
5.6.4 Violating Confidentiality.............................116
5.6.5 Jeopardizing Working Relationships............116
5.6.6 Violating Employee Rights...........................117
5.6.7 Vilifying Peers..117
5.6.8 Deliberately Underperforming....................118
5.6.9 Squashing Dissent......................................119
5.6.10 Ignoring Needs of Team Members...............119
5.6.11 Lacking Reliable, Consistent Treatment
       of Team Members...............................120
5.6.12 Not Encouraging Collaboration..................120
5.6.13 Dismissing without Cause...........................120
5.6.14 Sending a Defective Product to a
       Customer...121
5.6.15 Unauthorized Copying...............................121
5.6.16 Lacking Consistent Enforcement of
       Standards..122

5.7   Monitoring and Controlling and Ethics 122
      5.7.1   Misreporting 122
      5.7.2   Massaging or Not Sharing Information
              with Critical Stakeholders 124
      5.7.3   Not Using Reliable Data to Generate
              Information 124
      5.7.4   Not Using Plans to Report Progress 125
      5.7.5   Deliberately Not Reporting Bad News 125
      5.7.6   Inflating Expense Reports 126
      5.7.7   Destroying or Stealing Vital Information.... 126
5.8   Closing and Ethics 127
      5.8.1   Not Delivering Results as Promised 128
      5.8.2   Not Satisfying Contractual Requirements ... 128
      5.8.3   Falsifying Records 129
5.9   General Ethical Dilemmas 129
      5.9.1   People and Ethics 129
              5.9.1.1   Allowing a Toxic Culture to Exist 131
              5.9.1.2   Incivility 131
              5.9.1.3   Harassment 132
              5.9.1.4   Violation of Privacy 132
              5.9.1.5   Retaliation 132
              5.9.1.6   Coercion 133
              5.9.1.7   No Respect for Values 133
              5.9.1.8   No Provision of Honest
                        Feedback 134
              5.9.1.9   Treat People Inequitably 134
              5.9.1.10 Lack of Personal Responsibility.... 134
              5.9.1.11 Spread of Malicious Rumors 135
              5.9.1.12 Misuse of Power and Position 135
              5.9.1.13 Discrimination 136
              5.9.1.14 Encourage or Not Deal with
                        Infighting 136
              5.9.1.15 Not Treat Everyone Fairly and
                        Equitably 137
              5.9.1.16 Not Stopping Hidden Agendas 137
              5.9.1.17 Exploit People 138
              5.9.1.18 Deliberate Malicious Damage to
                        Reputations 138

5.9.2   Process and Ethics 139

     5.9.2.1   Receiving Inappropriate
             Entertainment and Gifts 139

     5.9.2.2   Conflict of Interest with
             Vendors and Suppliers 140

     5.9.2.3   Lacking Due Diligence and Due
             Care 140

     5.9.2.4   Massaging Feedback 141

     5.9.2.5   Unequal Access to Key
             Information and Other
             Resources 142

     5.9.2.6   Engaging in Illicit Activities 142

     5.9.2.7   Not Reporting Unethical
             Behavior 143

5.9.3   Performance and Ethics 143

     5.9.3.1   Revealing Privileged
             Information 143

     5.9.3.2   Not Confronting Problems
             Up Front 144

5.9.4   Perception and Ethics 144

     5.9.4.1   Deception 144

     5.9.4.2   Not Emphasizing the Overall
             Interests of a Project 145

     5.9.4.3   Deliberately Attempting to
             Damage Company Reputation
             and Product Image 146

5.10   Final Thoughts 146

5.11   Getting Started Checklist 147

Chapter 6   Ethics and Project Governance 151

6.1   What Is Governance? 151

6.2   What Are Controls? 153

6.3   What Is Risk? 153

6.4   Effective Risk Management 156

6.5   Final Thoughts 158

6.6   Getting Started Checklist 158

Chapter 7   Ethics and the Law 163

    7.1   The Relationship between Law and Ethics 163
    7.2   Key Legal Terms 166
    7.3   Key Legal Principles and Concepts 168
    7.4   Numerous Laws and Regulations 172
    7.5   Final Thoughts 178
    7.6   Getting Started Checklist 178

Chapter 8   Ethics, Globalization, and Project Management 187

    8.1   Important Factors 187
    8.2   Key Dimensions 188
    8.3   Independence, Integration, and Interdependence ... 189
    8.4   Challenges 191
    8.5   Breeding Ground and Consequences 194
    8.6   Key Actions 196
    8.7   Final Thoughts 198
    8.9   Getting Started Checklist 199

Chapter 9   Making Ethics a Reality 203

    9.1   Why Ethics Takes a Back seat 203
    9.2   Making Ethics on Projects a Reality 204
    9.3   The Mark of an Ethical Project Manager 206
    9.4   Getting Started Checklist 206

Glossary 207

Bibliography 213

Index 215

Preface

When people talk about *project management*, a discussion of ethics is rarely at the top of anyone's list. Procurement management, risk management, scheduling, and communications management, to name just a few, are all considered before there is any mention of ethics. Even on some certification exams it is treated as an ancillary topic. Yet ironically, an ethical violation is one of the quickest ways to destroy a project in general and a project manager in particular. Then, interestingly, topics like procurement management, risk management, and time management are somehow no longer important, and ethics becomes the center of discussion.

Ethics, therefore, is about choice—about becoming a topic worthy of attention and about making judgments and taking action to do what is ethical. You or your team members make a choice between what is and is not correct. Yet, while the choice is between right and wrong, the decisions and actions taken involve a considerable amount of gray. There is no algorithm to help you or any other project manager deal with issues about ethics with absolute assurance of effectiveness. About the most you can hope for is to make a judgment and act in a manner that resolves an issue equitably and honestly.

Ethics is not just for the big boys, either. Enron and other companies that joined its ranks may be titular examples of how poor ethical decisions and actions bring havoc on a wide range of stakeholders, from stockholders to employees. Ethics is also a concern for the people in the trenches who execute the strategies to produce a product or deliver a service. An ethical lapse can cost a corporation millions and frequently billions—all because a rank-and-file employee made or executed an unethical decision.

Many organizations may go through the motions of compliance training, but that is only one part of ethics and often gives people the illusion that they are ethical merely because they have been trained. Nothing is further from the truth. Just like taking a course on religion does not make you religious or completing a class on accounting does not make you a great accountant, ethics compliance, albeit necessary, is just one aspect.

Ethics must be total in thought and application if it is to be effective; anything less is compromise.

Let's say you are a project manager on a multimillion dollar project. For some companies that is a big project; for others it is small. Regardless, you have an ethical responsibility to your organization, to your project, and to yourself to take the high road, meaning that you have to do what's right. You will have to make judgments and take actions that will have ethical consequences on a constant basis. Straying from that road can negatively impact many areas—for example, people, performance, processes, perception, and profits (what I call the five Ps). Any ethical lapse will likely impact one, some, or all of these areas.

The pressures today are really no less than those in the past; however, they have taken a different form and provide opportunities for severe lapses in ethical judgment and actions in some very open and subtle ways. Some of those pressures include an unrelenting pressure to produce faster, better, cheaper; to manage projects and programs spread across the globe involving different cultures with varying perceptions about what is ethical; to lead projects in an environment where people can do great work and still find themselves without a job due to outsourcing; and experience an augmented regulatory oversight environment that may reveal events and activities which, up to this point in time, went undetected.

Ethics is what I call a positive negative: Good ethical behavior has positive consequences and is never appreciated and, therefore, gets no attention; lack of ethical behavior occurs and only then is appreciated because of the negative consequences that arise. It is like education; if you think it is expensive, then try ignorance and you'll see the costs. People have a tendency to view ethics as fluff and something that adds no value and, consequently, pay no attention to ethical judgments and behavior until something goes ethically awry and costs an organization, a project, and a person's career. Once the consequences become real, then suddenly ethics has value and then, sadly, it is often too late.

As a project manager and corporate auditor with a Fortune 500 firm spanning 25 years, I have reviewed and managed several ethics-related projects and programs at the strategic and operational levels. A strong argument can be made that ethics is equally important at both levels because an ethical lapse—either in judgment or action—occurs where the real work is done, where strategic dreams, so to speak, become operational realities. A poor decision on an ethical dilemma can wreck the best of intentions when tainted with poor judgment and behavior.

I also want to thank Ameeta Chianani for taking the time to review the manuscript and to provide insights on improving it.

Ralph Kliem
President, Lean PM, LLC
www.theleanpm.com
Ralph@theleanpm.com

About the Author

Ralph L. Kliem has more than 25 years of experience with Fortune 500 firms in the financial and aerospace industries. His wide, varied experience in project and program management includes managing compliance and information technology projects and programs.

In addition to being the author of more than 15 books, which have been translated in several languages, he has published more than 200 articles in leading business and information systems publications.

Mr. Kliem is an adjunct faculty member of City University in Seattle and a former member of the Seattle Pacific University faculty; an instructor with Bellevue College and Cascadia Community College; and a frequent presenter to the Puget Sound chapter of the Project Management Institute and other professional organizations. He also teaches Project Management Professional (PMP) certification and other project management seminars and workshops in the United States and Canada.

1

Ethics and Project Management

The subject of ethics, of course, is not a new one. It has been around for many centuries. Like the topic itself, circumstances dealing with ethics continue to resurface everywhere, often with disturbing repetitiveness. That goes for the project environment, too. Whether managing a large, medium, or small project, project managers will have to confront ethics on an ongoing basis.

1.1 WHAT IS ETHICS?

There are many different definitions of ethics:

- "Ethics refers to a systematic study of the norms and values that guide how humans should live their lives."[*]
- "[Ethics] is the activity of understanding moral values, resolving moral issues, and justifying moral judgments. It is also the discipline or area of study resulting from that activity."[†]
- "[Ethics is] a branch of philosophy dealing with values that relate to the nature of human conduct and values associated with that conduct."[‡]

---

[*] Joseph Desjardins, *An Introduction to Business Ethics*, 2nd ed. (Boston: McGraw-Hill, 2006), p. G3.

[†] Roland Schinzinger and Mike W. Martin, *Introduction to Engineering Ethics* (Boston: McGraw-Hill, 2000), p. 8.

[‡] David P. Twoney and Marianne M. Jennings, *Law and Business* (Australia: Cengage Publishing, 2008), p. G9.

- "The study of ethics generally consists of examination of right, wrong, good, evil, virtue, duty, obligation, rights, justice, fairness, and so on, in human relationships with each other and other living things."[*]
- "Ethics involves judgments about the rightness or wrongness of human behavior."[†]

These definitions seem to center around certain characteristics that are addressed by the topic of ethics in general:

- *Determining good from bad.* Frequently, that means choosing right from wrong. An example is determining when a particular action on your part or that of a team member needs to be addressed.
- *Judgment.* As a project manager, you often have to decide whether to make a decision about an ethical situation or whether to take action and to what degree. An example would be determining whether to elevate an ethical situation to higher management for resolution.
- *Behavior.* Ethical beliefs are exhibited values that are reflected through action. In other words, beliefs and values influence behavior. You and your team members reflect ethics through the ways you and the others make decisions and how you go about executing them. An example would be whether an ethical decision is made unilaterally or through the consultation of other team members.
- *Ethical situations.* Some of these situations involve dealing with adverse topics, adding a level of complexity that other project management topics address. For example, calculating earned value is straightforward; addressing a situation that injures a person's reputation is not that black and white.
- *Determining the appropriate response to a given situation.* This requires looking at a number of options and choosing the right one that effectively resolves an issue. Determining an appropriate response requires wrestling with issues like fairness, integrity, objectivity, honesty, and appropriateness. Tied closely to judgment, project managers must respond in such a manner that requires taking the high road, which in this case is choosing a response commensurate with the circumstances. An example is bringing attention to an

[*] Joanne B. Cuilla, *Ethics: The Heart of Leadership* (Westport, CT: Praeger, 1998), p. 4.
[†] Craig E. Johnson, *Ethics in the Workplace: Tools and Tactics for Organizational Transformation* (Thousand Oaks, CA: Sage Publications, 2007), p. xxii.

ethical issue that could result in angering certain key stakeholders even though you know you are right in doing so.

From the perspective of a project manager, ethics can therefore be defined as exercising objective judgment, after considering all options, on what is the right decision and response when dealing with ethical situations.

1.2 MISPERCEPTIONS ABOUT ETHICS

Applying such a definition in the real world of project management is not easy. In the contemporary environment, projects and team members find themselves in a fluid, dynamic realm that makes ethics a difficult topic to address. The pressure is immense to reduce costs and to meet an aggressive schedule and rigorous quality standards. This leads to opportunities to put ethics aside as a topic of serious consideration; it remains the case in many organizations, unfortunately. This happens for many reasons because there are some misperceptions surrounding ethics, some of which are described below.

1.2.1 Ethics Has No Bottom-Line Value

It is hard to fathom, but some people argue that the topic of ethics offers no value because it offers nothing tangible. Nothing could be further from the truth. Ethics offers nontangible and tangible value. From a nontangible value perspective, perhaps the most important benefit is that it provides a framework for making decisions and taking actions—not so much when the issues are easy to discern but when a confusing level of complexity exists. A strong sense of ethics enables project managers to make decisions and to take action to deal with the gray areas of ethical situations. These areas exist when right from wrong is unclear. From a tangible value perspective, perhaps the most important benefit is when ethics fails and the consequences become quite apparent. Disbarment from future contracts with the government and levy of civil and criminal fines on individuals and firms are tangible results. However, some findings suggest that ethics also leads to something else that is tangible: greater profits. From a project perspective, the tangible value is apparent through greater information sharing and collaboration among team members. When that fails to occur, especially when ethical circumstances deteriorate, project managers can see the result: slipped schedules, poor quality of output, and exceeding the budget.

1.2.2 Ethics Is an Abstract, Not a Real, Concept

This misperception is closely related to the previous point. The difference here is that people often construe ethics as important in a college course on philosophy but not in the real world when products are being produced and services are being delivered. According to some people, discussions of Socrates, Plato, and Joseph Campbell belong at the university and not in the work environment. Unfortunately, this misperception is shortsighted, leading to decisions and actions that can cause considerable real damage to a project and the company at large. For example, project managers who do not appreciate or understand the conceptual underpinnings of ethical theory will find themselves facing legal or even extralegal problems.

1.2.3 Ethics Is a Stand-Alone Topic

This means, of course, that it is a topic that has no relevance with others topics. Ethics permeates other topics and needs to be integrated with them. You cannot divorce ethics from risk management, time management, cost management, or any other topic related to project management. Project managers must, and often do without realizing it, incorporate ethics in their decisions and actions when managing and leading their projects. Project managers who do not consider ethics now will find themselves doing so later on, if and when ethical violations occur, for example, when executing a schedule and reporting on it.

1.2.4 Ethics Is Applicable to People Only at the Top of an Organization

It is convenient to come to this conclusion because often the news of an ethical transgression makes it to the headlines when it involves a chief executive officer (CEO) of a major corporation. Once again, nothing can be further from the truth. Ethics applies up and down the hierarchy, whether for projects at the executive or operational levels. Without one realizing it, the failure of ethics can have tremendous effects on a project or program without having to be immediate. For example, gratuities from a customer that exceed a certain value can affect objective decision making about the quality of output. This would result in long-term warranty costs and litigation from the public but would never make the headlines. Ethics applies not just to project managers but also to their team members. According to an allPM.com survey, project team members are "most likely" to recognize potential problems on a project. Those who fall within "least likelihood" are project managers, users, and senior managers.*

1.2.5 Ethics Applies to the Other Person

The same mind-set works here. Ethics involves someone else because my job is not as important or because there is less visibility in what I do. This misperception can lead to gross oversights in ethical behavior because it is perceived that everything about a project occurs under the radar. In reality, a lapse in ethics under these circumstances can result in ethical transgressions that can have negative impacts once discovered. What the public does not know won't hurt it, goes an old saying. But if the public does find out, all sorts of financial and legal problems could arise. Ethics applies to everyone, under all circumstances, regardless of scale and visibility.

1.2.6 Ethics Involves Only Compliance

If that were the case, ethics would be simply a matter of obeying laws and regulations. To a large extent, this view of ethics seems to prevail today. Unfortunately, it is a shortsighted one. True, fines and penalties can be severe, and public relations can become a disaster for a firm when an ethical transgression occurs. Compliance, however, is one sliver of the complex topic of ethics, especially on projects. Ethics covers character, integrity, honesty, fairness, and trust, to name just a few topics manifested through the decisions and actions involved in a given project. An unethical decision or action can affect how the team works together, its quality of output, and its treatment of the customer. Compliance is just one variable of the equation of ethics.

---

* "In Trouble," *PM Network* (September 2006), p. 16.

1.2.7 Ethics Deals Only with Matters That Are "Black and White" in Nature

Wrong. In fact, the argument can be made that if answers are as simple as being black and white (e.g., do this and don't do that), then ethics would be a no-brainer. But quite often, ethics deal with gray issues, ones where the decision or actions taken are not black and white and the consequences are unknown. Project managers, more often than not, deal with gray issues. For example, they have to make decisions and take actions related to negotiations with vendors. These decisions and actions could impair relationships or determine which data and information to share with partners, while simultaneously comply with intellectual capital requirements. Project managers frequently have to balance such decisions and actions while at the same time ensuring compliance with organizational policies and procedures.

1.3 KEY FACTORS

Project managers and their team members are influenced by many factors, spanning across the work and nonwork environment, in their definition and perception of ethics.

1.3.1 Peers

Whether in the work or nonwork environment, one of the strongest influences is peer relationships. In the nonwork environment, the peer influence can come from members of a professional society or a social networking group. It can even come from friends or acquaintances the project managers or their team members may have known over a period of time. In a work environment, it can come from fellow team members or other key stakeholders, such as a functional manager to whom they report directly.

One of the major sources of peer pressure can be from groups, informal as well as formal, in the workplace. Formal groups are the established organizations within an organization. These are people, by virtue of their position (e.g., executives, senior management), who are shown in a typical organization chart. In contrast, informal groups are not reflected in an organizational chart but have a powerful influence, sometimes more so than formal groups. These may be people of the same age group, people with a common background or trade, who share common interests. Informal groups can arise inside and outside the organization.

A project team often is a formal grouping of people to accomplish specific goals and objectives. Informal groups can transcend formal groups by involving relationships inside and outside the project. These relationships in informal groups can affect how people on a project work together. The challenge comes when the informal relationship become so intense that it may actually impede the performance of a project. For example, ethics transgressions can occur that can potentially put the project manager crosswise with the team.

1.3.2 Culture

Project managers and team members are strongly influenced by the cumulative beliefs, values, norms, mores, procedures, practices, stories, and habits that occur in their environment. Culture can sometimes become quite oppressive, influencing decisions and actions taken to deal with ethical dilemmas. A strongly autocratic, hierarchical organization can cause project managers and team members to circumvent controls, resulting in ethical transgressions that can in part provide an excuse for unethical decisions and actions. However, a strongly democratic organization can provide immense peer pressure. For example, groupthink can cause project managers and team members to make unethical decisions.

1.3.3 Power

As a British foreign minister in the early part of the previous century said, "Absolute power corrupts absolutely." Power can make people do things that they would not ordinarily do simply because the consequences of its exercise can become quite severe.

Power is the ability to influence means and outcomes, and it exists on an institutional and personal level. From an institutional standpoint, power can originate from the top, middle, and bottom layers. For example, power from the top can come from the board of directors; from the middle it could be senior management; and from the lower levels it could come from labor unions. From a personal perspective, power can take the form of five powers, as identified by the French and Raven* model: legitimate, reward,

---

* Rita Mulcahy, PMP Exam Prep, 6th ed. (Minnetonka, MN: RMC Publications, 2009), 236.

coercive, expert, and referent. For example, persons in a position of formal authority can exercise power due to their legitimacy within the organization; persons with reward power can influence outcomes through the use of incentives; or persons with a charismatic personality can dictate outcomes through the manipulation of others.

Ethics and power often go hand in hand because the latter can dictate the former. For example, the tone at the top can permeate the ranks of an organization. If the tone is negative, then ethical considerations could become a lower priority than if the tone is positive (not the same as permissive). Effective project managers are always attuned to the contextual atmosphere, both vertically and laterally. They know that a negative atmosphere can affect how decisions are made and what actions are taken to deal with ethical issues.

1.3.4 Competition

While competition offers many benefits, it also can lead to dysfunctional decision making and behavior on projects. Just to name a few, if not managed properly, competition can lead to accusatorial behavior, a win–lose perspective, a lack of sharing information, and a dearth of collaboration among stakeholders.

When competition becomes intense, just to get the advantage some people can start taking shortcuts that can lead to ethical transgressions. Power struggles can surface, thereby pitting one or more team members against another. Peer group pressures can cause talented people to leave, resulting in mediocrity, a result contrary to what competition is all about.

1.3.5 Rewards

Positive and negative rewards play an instrumental role in affecting ethical decisions and behavior. Rewards are perhaps one of the strongest influences on ethics. While positive rewards often have the intent of encouraging likewise behavior, sometimes just the opposite happens. The rewards can be so positive that people are willing to suspend ethical judgment and behavior on the simple notion that the gain will somehow compensate for the transgression. For example, a substantial bonus can cloud people's judgment and allow them to make questionable decisions. Negative rewards can also cause people to suspend ethical judgment and behavior to avoid pain, such as the loss of a contract or justifying lying to prevent penalties being levied against the company, thereby resulting in disbarment from participating in government contracts. Regardless of whether it is a positive or negative incentive, the potential for ethical problems can and often does arise.

1.3.6 Experiences

The past can become a great teacher; it can also set a bad precedent. Sometimes experience performing an ethical transgression can prove quite valuable, especially if it had gone undetected or was encouraged and involved no punishment. Under such circumstances, project managers may have survived one or two projects using ethical transgressions. Success in this regard does not justify such transgressions. Instead, it simply means that the project managers or team members did not "get caught." Examples include not reporting a problem and falsifying charging practices. Project managers may have decided to ignore the problem or simply covered up the situation. Regardless, their decision or action may have gone unnoticed, thereby encouraging them to behave similarly on a future project.

1.3.7 Role Expectations

On a project, everyone has a role, with some more important than others depending on the circumstances. Accompanying each role are expectations that may be set by other stakeholders or sometimes by a professional society or some other institution. Whatever the origins, the expectations can put a tremendous load on what that person is supposed to do or not supposed to do. Project managers are constantly placed in the unique position of having to fulfill the expectations of more than one stakeholder, which can put tremendous pressure on them with limited authority. Often, these expectations are formal.

In some circumstances, role expectations are not formal but informal, often based on the precedent of a predecessor or the general tone of higher management. For example, the project manager may be expected to prefer the stick over the carrot in motivating team members. Under such circumstances, if pressure exists then project managers may take unethical measures to remove a team member, through vilification or modifying reports to please certain powerful stakeholders.

1.3.8 Structure

The structure of an organization can influence ethical decision making and actions, particularly when an ethical transgression occurs. A centralized organization, for example, may assume all responsibilities for decisions and actions related to ethics, which can lead to an upward delegation of ethical responsibilities. This would allow, however unintentional, resulting in people awaiting a decision on dealing with an ethical dilemma. A decentralized organization, for example, has the potential opposite situation. The lower-level organizations may decide to keep ethical situations or transgressions under the radar, leaving the higher organization unaware of what is happening.

1.3.9 Management Style

The impact of management style can be hard to detect, yet it has profound consequences. Management style exercised throughout the ranks of an organization can influence ethical decision making and behavior. The tone at the top can influence ethics and can be reflected in formal documentation, including policies, procedures, and organization charts, or in the ways of doing business, including how management interacts with the rank and file and how it encourages problem solving.

Likewise, tone on the project can influence ethical decisions and behavior. A project manager's demeanor can sway the conduct of business, but so can the thoughts and behavior of the team and other stakeholders. For example, groupthink can become so strong that it can actually cause people to make decisions and act in ways that they would ordinarily not do, some of which result in ethical transgressions. According to a survey by Crucial Skills Newsletter, 78 percent of the respondents indicated that their current project is "doomed" and only about 10 percent felt they could freely discuss the dismal fate of their projects.*

1.4 COMMON TERMINOLOGY

Ethics, as defined in this book, is exercising objective judgment on what is the right decision and response when dealing with ethical situations after

---

* "We're All Doomed Unless You Start Talking," *PM Network* (June 2007), p. 18.

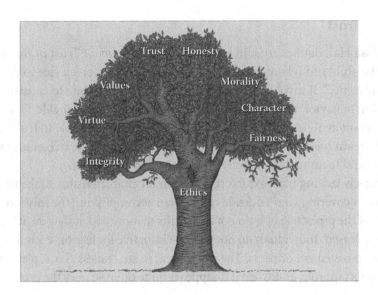

FIGURE 1.1
Ethics—common terminology.

considering all options. The topic of ethics involves a host of terminology that is highly interrelated and integrated. Some of the more common terms discussed in this chapter are *rights, loyalty, trust, morality, virtue, honesty,* and *integrity* (Figure 1.1).

1.4.1 Values

One of the essential elements of ethics is having a set of values to help you determine the appropriate decision and response to an ethical situation. Values, based on beliefs acquired over a period of time, help you to distinguish between good and bad or right and wrong. Values are really beliefs exhibited when dealing with ethical situations but also when conducting normal business. As Joseph DesJardins notes in *An Introduction to Business Ethics*, "Ethical values are those standards that include us to act in ways that impartially promote human well being."*

Often values are not clear-cut but overlap with one another, and this conflict surfaces when you must deal with an ethical decision. The conflict in values may be over how to resolve conflict among stakeholders or over how to communicate bad news that reflects negatively on the performance not only of the project but also of the project manager, too.

---

* DesJardins, *Introduction to Business Ethics*, p. G5.

1.4.2 Trust

Vanessa Hall defines trust in her book, *The Truth about Trust in Business,* as "the ability to rely on a person, company, product, or service to deliver an outcome."* It involves being able to depend on someone to consistently exhibit behavior that is honest, straightforward, and reliable. Trust is important at all levels of a project. Stakeholders must be able to trust each other, team members must be able to trust their project manager and vice versa, and team members must be able to trust each other.

Projects lacking trust exhibit some common characteristics. Stakeholders focus on covering your backside rather than accomplishing the mission and goals of the project. People do not share information, and, if they do, it is partially released. Individuals do not take the initiative for fear of reprisal either from management or peers. The consequences are endless. Trust plays such an important role, and when it disappears quite often so does the project.

1.4.3 Honesty

Dealing with ethical situations requires people being truthful in their interactions. People express themselves in a way that encourages further dialogue and fact finding in contrast to being evasive or telling only part of a story. As Stephen M. R. Covey in *The Speed of Trust* notes about honesty, "…[It] includes not only telling the truth, but also leaving the right impression. It's possible to tell the truth but leave the wrong impression. And that's not being honest."†

Honesty permeates everything in project management because the focus is on achieving results. The opposite of honesty—dishonesty—can have serious ramifications on a project. For example, playing with the numbers in a way that misleads key stakeholders about the performance of a project can result in the project manager losing credibility and can also impact the overall performance of the organization. Without honesty, trust declines.

1.4.4 Morality

Morality is a loaded term in just about any environment because of the subjective nature of the topic. Regardless, it is fair to say that it consists of the

---

* Vanessa Hall, *The Truth About Trust in Business* (Austin, TX: Emerald Book Club, 2009), p. 11.
† Stephen M. R. Covey, *The Speed of Trust: The One Thing that Changes Everything* (New York: Free Press, 2006), p. 62.

customers, habits, and values of a person or organization and is reflected in examining how it makes decisions and takes action when dealing with ethical situations. Notes DesJardins in *An Introduction to Business Ethics*, "Morality [refers] to those aspects of ethics involving personal, individual decision-making."* An important consideration when looking at morality is the degree to which a person or organization has a sensitivity to moral considerations. A high level of sensitivity is good; a low sense can lead to ethical transgressions.

Morality plays an important role on projects because it is exhibited in the way of doing business. If morality is low then trust, honesty, integrity, and fairness are just some of the victims. Backstabbing, finger pointing, information hoarding, and hidden agendas become the norm rather than the exception. As a result, a project is destined to fail under those circumstances.

1.4.5 Character

Character consists of many of the elements discussed already and essentially is the traits or qualities an individual or organization possesses that are exhibited when making decisions and taking action. Character is a key topic in leadership in general and ethics in particular. It is evident by exhibiting a standard of behavior.

Character on an individual basis has been discussed in leadership books across a wide spectrum of disciplines. Character is molded over time through the totality of knowledge and experience and provides a frame of reference for dealing with ethical situations. "The enduring marker or etched-in factors in our personality, which includes our inborn talents as well as the learned and acquired traits imposed upon us by life and experience. These engravings define us, set us apart, and motivate behavior," writes Joanne Ciulla in *Ethics: The Heart of Leadership.*† People are often described as having good, bad, strong, or weak character, and this influences how they will respond to an ethical situation. Clearly, persons of good or strong character will do what is appropriate and will take the high road; persons of bad or weak character will perform ethical transgressions.

Organizations have character, too, which is exhibited by the decisions and actions taken in response to ethical situations. Policies, procedures,

---

* DesJardins, *Introduction to Business Ethics*, p. G3.
† Cuilla, *Ethics*, p. 37.

norms, and morals give a strong indication of an organization's character. This trait is also exhibited through the tone at the top, that is, how the executive leadership conducts its business.

From a project management perspective, character is critical to the successful completion of a project. Project managers must possess an ethical character if they hope to be effective. Failure to exhibit good character can result in loss of credibility and trust with all stakeholders. Team members should possess good character; otherwise, a project will be plagued with overt and subtle problems related to human relations.

1.4.6 Virtue

Virtue is one of the traits or characteristics that make up the character of the individual or organization. A virtuous person, for example, is said to possess moral sensitivity, an internal moral framework, integrity, and trustworthiness. A virtuous organization shares many of the same traits or characteristics.

Virtue is exhibited through actions. It is not enough simply to claim to be virtuous. Virtues, a key element of character, are, according to Craig Johnson in *Ethics in the Workplace*, "deep rooted dispositions, habits, skills, or traits of character that incline persons to perceive, feel, and act in ethically right and sensitive ways."[*] It requires exhibiting traits or characteristics consistently when confronting ethical situations, especially difficult ones dealing with ethical transgressions. When ethical transgressions are obvious, such as a team member falsifying labor charging, it does not take much ethical fortitude to take appropriate action; it takes courage, however, to act ethically in response to an ethical situation where the issues are gray rather than black or white.

1.4.7 Fairness

Also known as equity, fairness involves being able to weigh the circumstances of an ethical situation when making a decision and taking action in a manner that is just to all parties. It requires, for example, creating a balance by distinguishing facts from assumptions to derive an equitable resolution to a problem. O. C. Ferrell, John Fraedrich, and Linda Ferrell

---

[*] Johnson, *Ethics in the Workplace*, pp. 41–42.

define fairness in *Business Ethics* as "the quality of being just, equitable, and impartial."[*]

Project managers exercise fairness throughout a project simply because they are often dealing with a large number of stakeholders and resolving conflict among them. This conflict may arise over schedules, resources, strategic priorities, or personalities, just to name a few. Project managers must balance interests in a way that hopefully results in a fair outcome for all parties, something akin to a win–win rather than win–lose result.

1.4.8 Integrity

Closely related to character, integrity is the manifestation of character. It is the cumulative beliefs and values of individuals, how they tie motive and action. There "...is no gap between intent and behavior," says Covey. "...When he or she is whole, seamless, the same—inside and out."[†] In other words, individuals with integrity walk the talk. Integrity is a window into the psyche of individuals and reveals their ethics, indicating just how much others can believe and trust them. People with integrity reflect a consistency between belief and values by always doing the right but not necessarily the easy decision or action required to address an ethical situation or transgression. When individuals lack integrity is when other people really appreciate its importance; you lose faith, trust, and credibility in them, and it is very difficult to restore. Sacrifice integrity, and project managers will experience the same fate and may never regain the faith, trust, and credibility of your stakeholders.

Not convinced that integrity is important? According to a recent survey by IBM, global senior leaders in the public and private sectors identified integrity as one of the top five leadership qualities over the next five years.[‡]

1.5 THEORETICAL UNDERPINNINGS

Although this book focuses on the practical application of ethics in a project environment, it is still important to understand at a rudimentary level the theoretical underpinnings behind the subject.

---

[*] O. C. Ferrell, John Fraedrich, and Linda Ferrell, *Business Ethics: Ethical Decision Making and Cases*, 6th ed. (Boston: Houghton Mifflin Company, 2006), p. 31.
[†] Covey, *Speed of Trust*, p. 62.
[‡] "The Leadership Track," *PM Network* (October 2010), p. 88.

The field of ethics goes back to the days of the Greeks and involves such notables as Plato, Socrates, and Aristotle, to name just a few. Questions of morality, justice, truth, honesty, virtue, and ethics commonly occupied their thoughts. In some cases, some ancient Greeks took their concepts to the extreme; for example, Diogenes walked around carrying a lantern looking for an honest man. To a large extent, with the exception of men like Diogenes, their focus in regards to ethics was based on the notion of moderation or balance, in what Aristotle referred to as the golden mean.

Over time, such discussion evolved into what is known as moral philosophy, that is, the purpose of morality with ethics becoming a major subject. Two camps arose in regards to ethics.

Deontological ethics is associated with one's particular behavior in regards to ethics. This behavior is based on universal truths or principles that identify what decisions and actions should and should not do. The focus is more on duty, exhibited through the adherence to these universal truths acquired through intuition or reason. Deontological ethics were best articulated by Immanuel Kant,* who developed the idea of categorical imperative, which essentially emphasizes duty and principles over other considerations (e.g., consequences). Project managers often get involved in deontological ethics. From an ethical perspective, some universal truths should be followed regardless of circumstances. For example, project managers should report honestly; they should treat all team members with respect; they should serve as trustees of a company's resources.

Teleological ethics emphasizes the desired results to achieve, that is, placing importance on the consequences when dealing with ethical situations. Utilitarianism is a common philosophy articulated by Jeremy Bentham and John Stuart Mills.† From an ethical perspective, the emphasis is on the consequences, for example, the greatest good for the greatest number or some other desired result. Project managers often get involved in teleological ethics. They have to deal with ethical situations. For example, they may have to deal with negative conflict among stakeholders and determine whose interests outweigh the others for the good of the project; they may have to weigh whether to develop in-depth plans is really necessary when considering the impact to the greater good of the project.

---

* DesJardins, Introduction to Business Ethics, 38-39.
† DesJardins, Introduction to Business Ethics, 87-90.

These two philosophical camps set the stage for a discussion of ethics, leading to more discrete perspectives on ethics, usually involving making a choice regarding ethical situations. These dilemmas include determining whether to emphasize the individual or the group, means or ends, determinism or free will, public versus private gain, and absolutism versus relativism.

One of the more contemporary ethical dilemmas is the discussion over ethical absolutism or ethical relativism and cultural centralism or cultural relativism. The fundamental issue surrounding ethical absolutism versus ethical relativism is whether certain ethical values are applicable universally across time and place or whether their application depends on circumstances. The fundamental issue surrounding cultural centralism versus relativism is whether one's own culture is superior and therefore exercised universally, whereas the cultural relativism entails not adhering to the idea that universal cultural beliefs and values exist. As globalism has an increasing presence, project managers will inevitably become involved with issues related to ethical and cultural absolutism and relativism and will have to determine whether, for example, their own cultural values take precedent over another culture or whether to adapt to another company's or country's ethical standards.

1.6 FINAL THOUGHTS

People have difficulty agreeing on the definition of ethics simply because of its abstractness. Yet, when an ethical failure occurs, everyone recognizes it as such; the consequences become tangible and real. The key is to have an agreed on definition and then to apply it to ethical situations and transgressions on your project. With that definition in hand, you will then be able to address ethical concerns with consistency, confidence, and competency.

1.7 GETTING STARTED CHECKLIST

	Question	Yes	No
1.	Whatever your definition of ethics, does it consider at least these characteristics?		
	Determining good from bad		
	Using judgment		
	Appropriate behavior		
	Addressing ethical situations		
	Providing appropriate responses to those ethical situations		
2.	Does your organization in general, and your project in particular, carry the following misperceptions about ethics? If so, are you going to do something about changing those misperceptions?		
	Ethics has no bottom-line value.		
	Ethics is an abstract, not a real, concept.		
	Ethics is a stand-alone topic.		
	Ethics is applicable to people only at the top of an organization.		
	Ethics applies to the other person.		
	Ethics involves only compliance.		
	Ethics deals only with matters that are "black and white" in nature.		
3.	Have you considered some of the following factors related to the definition and perception of ethics?		
	Peers		
	Culture		
	Power		
	Competition		
	Rewards		
	Experiences		
	Role expectations		
	Management style		
4.	Have you thought about how the following terminology applies to your own definition of ethics and that of your project?		
	Values		

Question		Yes	No
	Trust		
	Honesty		
	Morality		
	Character		
	Virtue		
	Fairness		
	Integrity		
5.	Does your application of ethics take one of two options?		
	Teleological		
	Deontological		

2

Why Ethics Should Matter
to Project Managers

Let's face it: Project managers have one of the hardest jobs in the world, simply because it is unique. In an age of specialization they are likely to be surrounded by people with a narrow disciplinary focus while they must have a broader perspective. Project managers work from a different—not necessarily higher—position that requires a different perspective. That's what makes them unique in one way. Other special circumstances, too, can contribute to ethical failure in judgment when dealing with ethical dilemmas.

2.1 UNIQUE CIRCUMSTANCES

Project managers work with different stakeholders, that is, persons or organizations that have a direct or indirect interest in the outcome of their project. They may deal with executives or managers from their organization or even those outside of it. They may deal with vendors or suppliers as well as people spanning a wide spectrum, from security to marketing to information systems and finance. This unique set of circumstances can cause ethical dilemmas to occur quickly easily. For example, some executives may be more powerful than the customer and, thereby, pressure the team or the project manager to put the customer's interests aside even though the customer is paying for the project. Unique circumstances may encourage team members to get too close with suppliers, thereby weakening or destroying objectivity and independence as well as reining the charge of conflict of interest when agreements are made with one vendor or another.

Chances are that project managers have responsibility without commensurate authority. Unless they find themselves in a "projectized" environment (meaning they have functional command and control over people, which is a rare circumstance), they are responsible for a work statement for which they have little or no control over the resources. This is often the case in a matrix environment, whereby the project manager relies on functional management and the sponsor to garner the financial or in-kind support to help complete a project. Such pressure can lead to actions, such as mischarging, to move the project along rather than to adhere to established policies and procedures by following labor charging practices or management's direction.

Another unique characteristic of a project is the pressure to achieve results in a relatively short period of time. Project managers and their team have to deliver a product or service in a prescribed time period. In the contemporary environment, that is not an easy task. In an age of faster, better, and cheaper, especially in the hi-tech arena, delays can be costly. Managers have to be quick and accurate from technical, cost, and schedule perspectives. Any delay can have negative impacts for the project and the company. This places immense pressure on project managers and their team. Since they likely do not have command and control over resources, the ground has potentially been laid to cut corners, which, in turn, can cause ethical situations and ethical transgressions to occur. For example, project managers or their team may decide to reduce the quality via a quick fix even though everyone knows of the long-term consequences to the public.

Still another unique position of project managers is that though the project is short-term many of their decisions can have long-term consequences. Whatever managers and their team decide today will likely have an impact on the project some time after delivering the product or service to the customer. A decision to change scope or content of the product or service, even if it goes under change control, will likely have an impact throughout the supply chain at one time or another. Developing new drugs is a prime example where, despite rigorous testing, without even realizing it a decision can lead to harmful effects, such as birth deformities. This unique circumstance can lead to ethical failure because the pressure is to deliver by a certain date and within a certain cost. Some project managers can become so focused that they make a decision to meet immediate needs only to discover later on, usually from the customer or product manager, the decision's negative ramifications.

Temporary relationships are another unique circumstance of a project manager. By its very nature, a project is temporary, and what comes with it are relationships. Team members come together hopefully with a common purpose, and once achieved they go back to their organizations or on to another project. Relationships are usually temporary, both during and after a project. Because of that very impermanence, some team members may either feel that the consequences of their actions don't matter or may just not care. Thus, they may say or do something that can be an ethical transgression. It is similar to someone doing something in another neighborhood such as littering and then returning to their own, confident that they do not need to face the consequences. Some project team members can have that attitude, particularly in a matrix environment, predicated on the rationale that they can return to their home organization or go work on another project.

Another unique circumstance of project managers is that they often work in different environments. Some have experience in project management in both business and technical environments. Project management is one such skill. The challenge is that what is permissible or acceptable in one environment may not necessarily be so in another, even within the same organization. Variables such as tone at the top, managerial style, and way of doing business can vary from one field to another. While this versatility enables managers to adapt, they can sometimes misinterpret or miscalculate circumstances, resulting in an inadvertent ethical transgression. An example may be managing a project outside the United States and then managing one in the United States. What is acceptable for doing business in one country may not necessarily be so in another. Laws and cultural behavior often conflict between two countries, leading to an ethical transgression in one but not in the other.

Project managers find themselves in circumstances that can, even in the most subtle ways, cause ethical situations and transgressions to arise. The challenge is to be aware of those circumstances and to determine the most appropriate ways to deal with such occurrences. Of course, the general business environment does not help matters either. Often there are circumstances beyond the control of project managers but that are not unique to the project environment, including rapidly changing conditions related to the market, domestic and international laws and regulations, political conditions, exchange rates, technology, consumer behavior, capital availability, stock market performance, and general economic conditions such as inflation or deflation. Such circumstances can lead to ethical lapses.

For example, a rapid change in political conditions may lead members of a global project to start spreading negative rumors about a member of a certain nationality working on their team. Or currency fluctuations can cause budgetary belt tightening for some projects without a corresponding slimming of scope, thereby laying the groundwork for mischarging or delivering a product that fails to meet standards without any knowledge of its poor quality until long after the project ends.

In these circumstances, coupled with a contemporary general business environment that seems lax from an ethics perspective, the opportunity for ethical failure does not seem too far-fetched. Surveys have pointed out the general laxity that exists in American culture. Several surveys by the Ethics Resource Center of the Society for Human Resource Management indicate that the following ethical failure (used in the context of infractions, from most to least as percentage of responses) by colleagues are: lying to supervisors; falsifying records; alcohol and drug abuse; stealing or theft; and gift receipt, caused primarily by considerable pressure to achieve financial or business objectives.* In a survey conducted by the Ethics Officer Association, close to 50 percent of the respondents noted that they had done something illegal or unethical in their organizations.† Interestingly, in a study on the United States by a British sociologist 76 percent of employees saw something illegal or unethical while at work.‡

When considering these special and general circumstances, it is quite clear that project environment is a potential hotbed for unethical behavior. Project managers must deal with a plethora of ethical issues and at any given time and place can find themselves dealing with an ethical situation or transgression related to a particular topic.

2.2 HARD AND SOFT ETHICAL ISSUES

While the list of ethical dilemmas is innumerable and overlap with each other in many respects, most can be divided into two general ethical categories: hard and soft. Hard ethical issues can have legal and financial

---

* O. C. Ferrell, John Fraedrich, and Linda Ferrell, *Business Ethics: Ethical Decision Making and Cases*, 6th ed. (Boston: Houghton Mifflin Company, 2006), p. 13.
† Ibid.
‡ Stephen M. R. Covey, *The Speed of Trust: The One Thing That Changes Everything* (New York: Free Press, 2006), p. 11.

No Commitment, Responsibility, & Accountability	Repressive Culture	Performance Pressure	Competing Priorities	Poor Communication	Not Balance Short & Long Term Perspective
Insider Trading	Dysfunctional Motivation	Extreme Behavior	Inadequate Reporting	Unfair Competitive Advantage	Breach of Contract & Agreements
Arbitrary Employment at Will	Lack of Employee Rights	Inadequate Health & Safety	Bribes & Kickbacks	Conflicts of Interest	No Due Care
Substandard Quality	No Due Diligence	Padding	Mischarging	Legal Noncompliance	Low Balling

FIGURE 2.1
Common issues involving ethics.

ramifications and are often quite apparent when a transgression occurs. Soft ethical issues can also have financial and legal consequences but are often difficult to determine in their occurrence and how to deal with them (Figure 2.1). What follows are some common hard ethical issues on projects.

Legal noncompliance is an issue that often gets the most attention because failure to comply has severe impacts, such as criminal and civil penalties, which can be applied to organizations and individuals alike. Ensuring adherence to laws and regulations, such as Sarbanes-Oxley, Sherman Anti-trust Act, and environmental laws, becomes absolutely essential to avoid penalties and bad public relations. Project managers and their team members can find themselves legally liable for failing to comply with laws and regulations, especially if their actions are not an expression of due diligence and due care. In recent years, legal and regulatory actions have pushed projects to start implementation of project management disciplines, if for no other reason than that stakeholders are seeking to protect themselves.

No due diligence and due care is one that is related to legal compliance. Due diligence is establishing standards, procedures, and responsibilities to prevent illegal and unethical behavior; due care is taking all the reasonable and necessary precautions to preclude harm. It is the result of due diligence being applied in reality through consistent activity and follow-up. Failure to take "reasonable" behavior and action to prevent harm can, from a legal perspective, place all stakeholders in harm's way.

Arbitrary employment at will is another one that involves deals with the contractual relationship between employees and their employers. Often issues concern the use of certain people based on their contract and their being removed from a project. Depending on the contractual provisions, dismissal has to be handled very carefully. How people are hired or released from a project depends not only on whether they are consultants or contractors but also on whether labor agreement restrictions exists as well as aspects of equal opportunity and affirmative action.

Lack of employee rights covers a wide breadth of topics and includes right to privacy, such as use of equipment for personal means, and intellectual property, such as who owns what if a project results in a patent. Employee rights can be a very murky issue in the project environment since in many cases contract employees and consultants are used. In some cases, how these two categories of workers are applied on a project can have, for example, tax and benefit consequences for an employer.

Inadequate employee health and safety can have a big impact on a project's work environment. Projects must often, for instance, focus on issues like carpel tunnel syndrome, hazard material (hazmat) handling of substances, construction of facilities such as lead and asbestos poisoning, and workplace violence.

Breach of contracts and agreements involves negotiating contracts or enforcing compliance with contracts both from a buyer and seller perspective. Project managers must also provide the necessary oversight and, if necessary, terminate a relationship for breach of contract. Agreements, of course, might include a project charter and memorandums of understanding.

Bribes and kickbacks are quite common and are hard to prove. A bribe or a kickback is used to eradicate impartiality in any decision-making process or to obtain favorable treatment in exchange for something of value. Project managers of projects that serve as prime contractors or manage a government project must be aware of the potential for bribes and kickbacks to arise.

Conflicts of interest can challenge an employee's allegiance to an organization. Even the mere appearance of a conflict of interest can be a serious ethical issue. Project managers must always be on guard for themselves and others on their team for potential and actual conflicts of interest. For example, employees on a project who participate in a negotiated contract with a company in which they own stock have a conflict of interest.

Mischarging deals with whether team members charge their work or services to the appropriate project and even to the right activity within a project. Mischarging can become serious business when customers or clients end up getting billed for work that they did not contract for and will not benefit from. In a matrix environment, team members on a project may support several projects, some of which are overhead and some of which are directly billable to the customer. Especially on the latter projects, ethical lapses can arise related to mischarging, such as wrongfully billing the government when the work was being done for a private customer or client.

Padding and low-balling can also occur. Padding occurs when estimates are artificially inflated for no other reason than to compensate for unknowns. The trouble with padding is that it is not based on sound reasoning and can lead to overcharging the customer or client for work that is not really done. Low-balling is getting a contract with a customer by deliberately underbidding to get the contract and then jacking up costs once the contract has been signed. While both padding and low-balling are not in themselves illegal, they can have unethical implications for projects. The reasons for this are many, but perhaps the most important one is that the contract was not negotiated in good faith. If the customer or client finds out about padding or low-balling, trust among all the stakeholders can quickly deteriorate, making management of any project difficult.

Insider trading involves people within a corporation sometimes having access to privileged information. Sometimes the temptation is very strong to use that information to their advantage, such as buying or selling stock either of their firm or another company. Stakeholders on a project that may involve making a major procurement agreement with another company could have a substantial impact on the price of its stock. This may tempt some team members to use that information to purchase additional shares of stock.

Substandard quality may at first not seem like it would involve an ethical situation or transgression, it certainly can have an impact if team members on a project deliberately fail to comply with standards and requirements. Sometimes, under cost and schedule pressures, team members may circumvent standards to meet the schedule. This circumvention may not be apparent at first; however, after project completion it could have severely negative effects, such as during sustaining and maintenance operations of the product. Knowingly allowing substandard quality workmanship to occur can mean not only more warranty costs but also those related to litigation.

Inaccurate reporting, perhaps from a project management perspective, involves one of the most common occurrence of ethical situations and transgressions. There are many reasons for this occurrence, especially in projects that face an environment of being faster, better, and cheaper. A tendency exists to "massage" the numbers or to communicate them in such a way that trivializes their impact. A key stakeholder, such as an executive, may take the numbers and then run with only one side of the story to satisfy some political requirement. Others may report negative information and then alter the results because there "is something wrong with the data." Especially on projects involving intense emotions, a strong tendency exists among people to hear what they want to hear and not what they need to hear. This situation is especially the case where metrics, such as earned value, are lacking on a project instead using subjective analysis, such a color-code screen. For example, three colors—red, yellow, and green—are used to report progress. Not supported by numbers, the project manager may decide to assess the color of the project as green even though everyone knows the schedule status is red, cost status is yellow, and technical quality is red. This is called *watermelon* reporting, because everything is green on the outside but a different color, such as red, on the inside. The project manager may be falsely reporting for all sorts of reasons, but regardless, it borders on being unethical, especially if he or she knows the true status but reports otherwise.

Unfair competitive advantage involves stakeholders seeking information that gives them an opportunity to wipe out the competition to win a major contract. Stakeholders may get an advanced copy of a competitive bid prior to submittal or hire people from a competitor and pressure the new hires to share privileged information from a previous employer that results in gaining an advantage. Project managers may face such pressures if the contract is quite lucrative to their organization or that it means the continuation of an existing contract. Such actions are not just unethical but are illegal, too.

Soft ethical issues on projects are more difficult to identify, but are significant:

Unbalanced short- and long-term perspectives entails project managers deciding to do a quick fix to get them out of trouble in the short-term, knowing that it will cause severe problems once the project is over. In other words, they knowingly pass on the problem, and perhaps a bigger one, to someone else, such as a product manager or maybe even the customer.

No commitment, responsibility, and accountability is another common ethical issue. Commitment is following through on what was promised; responsibility is carrying out a commitment; and accountability is holding oneself responsible for the results achieved. The ethical issue here is promising more than what can be delivered, not delivering as promised, and not taking responsibility for the results. Too often, especially in the beginning of a project, sometimes by design and sometimes by accident key stakeholders (who include project managers and team members) overcommit themselves, thereby later dashing customer expectations. Sometimes project managers commit to a schedule that is totally unrealistic. They commit to it, but when it is delivery time and a key milestone slides they are the first to put the blame on another stakeholder or some other contributor, thereby shirking responsibility and accountability.

Repressive culture exists in some environments where the culture can become so dominating that no matter what project managers do or say their insights are ignored. Culture, as mentioned in the last chapter, is reflected in the ways of doing business, from decision making to taking action. Extreme pressure can be exerted by senior leadership, so much so that the existence of ethical lapses are inevitable. Such conditions can put project managers and other project professionals in an ethical precarious position. The culture ranges from limiting a project manager's options to changing reports to reflect a story that does not exist.

Extreme behavior involves people exhibiting behavior that reflects their beliefs, values, priorities, and overall character. In some environments the only acceptable behavior is the one that aligns with the culture. For example, autocratic, even aggressive behavior by senior management may permeate to the project level, resulting in people not sharing information or keeping to themselves. Collaboration, communication, and coordination become the exception rather than the rule. Project managers who fail to exhibit such behavior can be construed as weak or not playing the game. Executive management, however, is not solely to blame; some project team members may be less than ethical, too. According to a survey by the Ethics Resource Center, misconduct has grown between 2000 and 2007. The survey noted that close to 60 percent of people have seen ethical misconduct occur in their workplace.*

---

* David McCann, "And Not a Moment Too Soon," *CFO* (January 2008), p. 17.

Dysfunctional motivation can arise when positive and negative incentives can propel a project to a successful conclusion but can also inadvertently encourage behavior that leads to ethical situations and transgressions. Positive incentives reinforce or encourage desirable behavior; negative ones concentrate on avoiding penalties. Incentives, of course, can also be financial and nonmonetary in nature—the former being an award for outstanding performance and the latter the opportunity for greater visibility for an advancement. Regardless of how classified, sometimes incentives encourage the wrong behavior. For example, an award given to certain team members may encourage backstabbing and other negative behavior from other team members. Some team members may alter reports to give the impression that performance is better than what it really is; others may perform lower during the day and work harder in the evening to be paid at higher rates, thereby inflating project costs.

Performance pressure is another common ethical issue. Crashing and fast tracking are two examples that place considerable pressure on projects to perform according to expectations. The pressure can come from many directions. As mentioned previously, project managers and other stakeholders may find it necessary to cut corners to meet cost or schedule targets or both, which may result in future problems long after completing a project. Pressure can be good, but there is a certain threshold that, once broken, will cause people to do what they can to survive. Some of these actions include finger pointing, shirking responsibility, sabotaging other people's work, and vilifying the character of some people. Interestingly, planning itself can be a major pressure cooker for project managers. According to an online survey by the Project Management Institute (PMI), for project managers planning is the most stressful process, followed by, from most to least, execution, monitoring and controlling, initiating, and closing.*

Competing priorities also confront stakeholders. Some of them feel their priorities are more important than others. To some stakeholders cost is more important; other stakeholders may feel that the schedule is important. Still others might emphasize quality. The problem is that project managers must constantly reconcile all these and other factors (e.g., scope and risk). Trying to resolve prioritization may lead to making decisions that could unfairly impact the expectations of a stakeholder. If people fail to inform a specific stakeholder that expectations will not be met, the level of trust and integrity afforded to the project

---

* "Hot July Button," *PM Network* (July 2007), p. 14.

manager could be negatively impacted. Dealing with the varying priorities of different stakeholders is one of the hardest tasks of a project manager. Of course, project managers should always decide in favor of the customer.

Poor communication is one of the most prevalent soft ethical issues. According to the PMI, project managers communicate 90 percent of their time with other stakeholders. If that is the case, it is quite clear that project managers should do nothing to hurt their credibility. When communicating, therefore, they should be open and responsive to questions and insights. Communications should be vertical and horizontal so that no one feels out of the loop. Project managers who fail to tell the truth stand a good chance of being discovered by the recipients and thus ruining their integrity. Honest and open communications, short of privileged information, should be a cardinal rule. Project managers who lose credibility will lose the project.

2.3 CONSEQUENCES OF ETHICAL FAILURE

When ethical dilemma arise, project managers need to take them on directly. Failure to act can have severe consequences.

Tarnished reputation is one consequence. If ethical transgressions go unaddressed, some stakeholders may not hold the project manager, the project, or the organization in very high regard. Managers will then find it difficult to get the support required to complete the project because people have lost faith in delivering what was promised.

Tarnished credibility is another consequence. Credibility is extremely important, and not just the project manager's. Team members need to maintain their credibility with other stakeholders because they are representatives of the project. Managing a project with little or no credibility can only result in poor outcome for the project.

Hindered careers can have an impact. An ethical situation or transgression left unattended can cause people to construe project managers as being weak, lacking ethical character, or simply being neglectful about something that should have been stopped.

Legal consequences is the final one. If the project manager, as either a participant or a witness, knows an ethical situation or transgression has occurred and does nothing to rectify it, he or she could experience legal recourse. Project managers are responsible for the overall performance of the team; allowing ethical situations or transgressions is, in many regards, a failure in due diligence, due care, and, most importantly, leadership.

2.4 CLOUDY PERSPECTIVE

Dealing with ethical failure is one of the most difficult responsibilities that project managers have to perform. The project environment frequently requires making tough decisions. The toughest are the ethical ones, often because the decision and action of dealing with an ethical situation or transgression is hardly straightforward. Short of something blatant—overt bribery or mischarging, for instance—acquiring a clear picture based on facts and data is difficult to achieve. Often, project managers have to shift through a sea of subjectivity, half-truths, and assumptions treated as facts and data. There are several reasons for this difficulty.

One, project managers, like everyone else, are a product of their background. Whether they admit it, their prejudices, especially when dealing with people issues, can cloud their judgment without really knowing it. A kind of value screen sometimes filters out the data of a given situation, resulting in a biased result. For example, a project manager who is highly experienced in a specific discipline may run a project in another new field of endeavor, in which certain facts and data about an ethical transgression are overlooked and, consequently, not considered when making a judgment.

Two, as much as project managers may try, they will find that they cannot release themselves from their current time and place. The pressures, some overt and many subtle, will influence their attempt to be objective in making a decision about and acting on an ethical situation or transgression. Both the internal and external environment can have a major impact on their thought processes. For example, the temper of the times in the past might be considered an ethical transgression, but in the current environment it is no longer considered very important.

Three, project managers may never have enough facts and data or may have a lot of both. However, neither one may suffice because the known facts and data may be only partial. Indeed, what is construed as a fact or datum is a really a human deconstruction of phenomena in the world and attempting to put what we know in human terms. This very act is, by its nature, subjective, especially when dealing with issues related to the human race. By deriving a fact or datum, project managers are by the very act deciding to exclude other considerations they deem either as insignificant or as an assumption.

Four, dealing with ethical situations and transgressions may require collecting facts and data, but in the end it calls for judgment over determining what is right and wrong. There are many schools of thought about whether there are absolute or relative truths when discussing ethics, but it is clear that ethics requires making one or more judgments that are, by their very nature, subjective. For example, what is the difference between a minor ethical transgression and a major one? Oftentimes, the line of demarcation is unclear.

Five, a key consideration when addressing an ethical situation or transgression is the frame of reference. This is like a paradigm or model on how project managers view the world. It determines what they deem is important and, conversely, unimportant. It is what they determine are the priorities, facts, and data in a given circumstance. It helps them deal with ambiguity but at a cost—introducing a bias that affects their objectivity. The challenge is to rise above the constraints of their paradigm, to make a decision and take an action, or both to make a fair judgment.

The influence of a paradigm will affect what is referred to as ethical consciousness—that is, what project managers believe is moral, immoral, or amoral. In a sense it serves as a moral compass that helps to distinguish among the three and then to make an appropriate decision about or taking action.

Regardless of the paradigm, project managers will find that they are likely to have to face an ethical situation or transgression more often than they wish. Probably most of the ethical decisions and actions are really quite simple; that is, the ethical steps to take are quite clear. In other words, the answer is between black and white. It does not really present a challenge.

2.5 THE ETHICAL DILEMMA

The challenge occurs when project managers face an ethical dilemma. That is, they have to make a decision and action that goes down one path or the other. Either way, positives and negatives exist, and there is no choice but to choose one. Everything then becomes a matter of gray rather than black and white. In other words, project managers face an ethical moment of truth, which then becomes a test of character.

Of course, when dealing with such situations they will use their beliefs and values, moral standards, and sense of what is right and wrong to help them discern the appropriate decision or action when dealing with an ethical issue or transgression. But that may not help managers to overcome the moral conflict rattling through their brain.

An ethical dilemma is tough. A typical one requires them to make a choice to do something (i.e., take action), referred to in this book as Path A, or not do something, Path B (Figure 2.2). Path A involves taking action, perhaps in a proactive way—something that resolves a potential ethical situation. Going down Path A has its merits; it may also have its costs. For example, a project manager may decide to do something to preclude an ethical situation occurring on her project. Such an action demonstrates the value she puts on a certain action and to reduce the risk that something might happen. It also involves incurring up-front costs. Nothing comes free.

Path B involves deciding not to take action to deal with a potential ethical situation or transgression. Going down path B has its merits; it may have its costs, too. For example, a project manager may make no decision or take no action to deal with a possible ethical situation or transgression. The positive is that by making no decision or taking no action, he gives the circumstance time to work itself out; if it should occur, possibly no one will find out. The negative side is that the situation occurs and goes beyond his control.

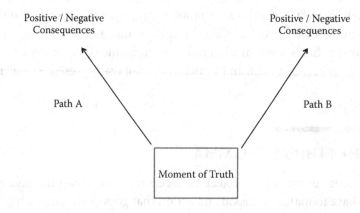

FIGURE 2.2
The great dilemma.

Picking Path B over Path A does not necessarily mean tolerating unethical decisions and actions—quite the contrary.

Picking Path B simply means it is a strategy for dealing with the possibility that an ethical situation or transgression may occur. If one or the other occurs, the ethical situation or transgression may not be serious enough to require making a choice. Choosing Path A or Path B, therefore, requires judgment. So what are the considerations for choosing Path A or Path B?

2.6 TWO KEY CONSIDERATIONS

There are two major considerations when dealing with an ethical dilemma: (1) the sensitivity of the issues; and (2) the intensity of the response. Both play an integral part in assessing and dealing with ethical failures (Figure 2.3):

1. Sensitivity of issue: Sometimes an ethical situation or transgression may not warrant the attention it deserves; other times it does. In other words, not all ethical situations and transgressions are equal. You have to determine the gravity of the situation or transgression, which will help you to decide on the appropriate response. For example, you figure out that one of the team members "fudged" his reporting but it did not have a material impact on the reporting.

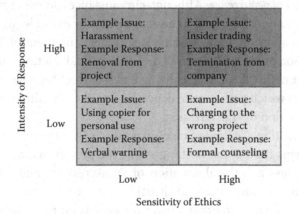

FIGURE 2.3
Intensity-sensitivity matrix (example).

2. Intensity of response: Some responses have greater weight than others; in fact, some could be overkill for the nature and type of an ethical situation and transgression that has occurred. A response is a conscious effort to make or not make a decision or act. Using the example in the previous paragraph, the project manager decides simply to talk to the person who "fudged" his reporting rather than elevate it up to his management.

Several factors should be considered when deciding both the sensitivity of an ethical situation or transgression and its intensity of response:

- *Magnitude of issue:* Is it a major ethical concern or a minor one? Obviously, if it is a blatant violation of the law or can result in damaging other people to a significant degree, it surely is a major ethical situation or transgression and requires action. If, on the other hand, it involves something minor like running a single paper copy of a personal nature on a company copier, it may not warrant taking action at all.

- *Scalability of issue:* Does the issue concern one individual or a large number of people? Of course, the involvement of one person may be of significance if, for example, that person is embezzling money from the company. However, if the person is doing something like taking an hour off without telling anyone on a periodic basis it may not impact anyone, and addressing the issue may create more problems than it is worth.

- *Context of occurrence:* Although circumstances do not excuse unethical behavior, they need to be examined. For example, was the ethical situation or transgression done under a moment of duress and fear? Sometimes people make decisions and take action, doing something unethical without realizing it at the time. The project manager decides which path to take depending on the magnitude of the ethical situation or transgression.

- *Ramification of actions:* Sometimes taking an action may cause more problems than doing nothing at all. The project manager may elect to address an ethical situation or transgression, and the very act itself may cause an ethical situation or transgression. He may hear a rumor circulating that a team member is doing something inappropriate; he also may know that the person is unpopular on the team and that the comment could possibly be an effort to impugn the person's character. Taking Path A could turn what was a minor issue into a major event that alienates the entire team.

- *Control over the situation:* The origins for the unethical behavior may be beyond the project manager's area of control. She may have some control or none at all. Her power to determine whether to pursue Path A or Path B may be minimal. For example, the tone at the top may be so overwhelming that she may find that addressing an unethical decision or taking an action is irrelevant.

- *Accident or design:* Sometimes, ethical situations and transgressions occur without any deliberate intent, such as a failure to report a minor wrongdoing. Sometimes, they occur by design, such as deliberately producing false reports. In most cases, if an ethical situation or transgression occurs by design the project manager needs to make a decision and take action.

- *Facts and data:* Oftentimes, emotions run high when ethical situations and transgressions occur. People can begin to lose trust and get defensive; some may start pointing fingers; others may decide to even get violent, emotionally or physically. You need to keep your cool and determine the who, what, when, where, why, and how about an ethical situation. Facts and data are critical to understanding the causes and impacts of an ethical situation or transgression because they help in allaying the emotion and subjectivity surrounding their occurrence.

- *Impact to stakeholders:* An ethical situation or transgression will have a varying impact on stakeholders; in other words, some will be more impacted than others. It is best for project managers to determine that impact beforehand so they can hopefully determine the cause and possible solution for dealing with the ethical issue and transgression. Through involvement, they will reduce resistance to any decision or action to address an ethical situation or transgression.

- *Consequences:* The impact will determine whether the ethical situation or transgression is severe enough to warrant attention and, just as importantly, what the appropriate response should be. In other words, the penalty, as an old saying goes, should fit the crime. You want to avoid overkill; otherwise, addressing the issue could introduce problems that are far more difficult to handle.

- *Assumptions:* A tendency exists to treat assumptions as facts. Often, this treatment is done out of ignorance or convenience because it requires time and effort to do so. Sometimes, too, time is not available, which causes people to jump prematurely to conclusions.

Assumptions are often intertwined with rationalizations, making it very difficult to distinguish fact from fiction. Failure to verify assumptions can make it difficult for you to acquire a clear understanding of the causes of ethical situations and transgressions and develop an appropriate response.

- *Causes:* Determine the causes of an ethical situation and transgressions. When project managers clearly identify the causes, they can then determine an effective response. They want to avoid a response that will only aggravate the circumstances or that fails to resolve the issue. Because emotions are high concerning ethical situations and transgressions, they can easily find themselves in a defensive position, especially if the decision or action they take or don't take is the wrong response.

- *Impact of response:* If project managers decide to respond, they can expect some type of pushback, especially from people who may benefit from an ethical situation or transgression. They cannot avoid it. They can even expect resistance from not doing anything because some people will find that the ethical situation or transgression hurts their interests. The main idea here is TANSTAAFL ("There ain't no such thing as a free lunch"). Whatever the manager's response, even if it means not making a decision or taking action, positive and negative consequences should be expected.

Both the sensitivity of the issue and the intensity of response require making a judgment; no cookie-cutter approach exists. This judgment requires looking across a continuum that moves from doing the minimum, balanced, to maximum; the boundaries overlap, indicating that project managers will always have to make judgments and adjustments depending on the circumstances (Figure 2.4). An example of a minimum

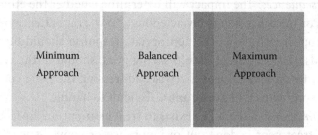

Minimum Approach   Balanced Approach   Maximum Approach

FIGURE 2.4
Judgment continuum.

approach is simply asking the person to stop committing the ethical transgression. A balanced approach is to have a more in-depth conversation about the reasons not to commit the transgression. The maximum approach is to elevate the issue to management and request a reprimand.

2.7 SENSITIVITY OF ISSUE

For ascertaining the sensitivity of issue, you can:

One, determine if an ethical issue or transgression has in fact occurred. Sometimes, what may look like one is really the result of an oversight or accident. It makes no sense to treat something as an ethical situation or ethical transgression when it really isn't one. Everyone just becomes alarmed and then will focus on protecting themselves rather than on completing their work. If the issue isn't an ethical transgression, it can be treated the same as any other problem or issue.

Two, assuming it is an ethical issue, then determine its sensitivity. The more sensitive the ethical issue or transgression, the more immediate attention it will require. As discussed earlier, an issue of law, such as someone receiving kickbacks, requires more attention than someone who runs a handful of copies for a religious group on the company copier. Good judgment should be used, because once something is given attention it has several consequences: Project managers will likely strain their relationship with the individual; they may end up imperiling the productivity of that individual; or they may encourage a subtle or overt retaliation. While ideally ethical issues or transgressions should never be tolerated, the reality is that managers cannot constantly fight them all; otherwise, all their attention and energy as well as that of team members, will be dissipated. Managers need to pick their battles when it comes to ethical issues and transgressions.

Three, identify the stakeholders involved in an ethical situation or transgression. Project managers need to know who committed it and who is impacted by it. Just as important is that they need to know why the person did it and how the others were impacted. They will need to know this information because it will help them, should they be assigned the responsibility to conduct investigation behind the causes and to determine if this has been a consistent pattern. If someone else does the investigation, such as an investigator responding to a hotline call, managers may likely have to provide this information anyway.

Four, conduct the inquiry to collect the relevant facts and data related to the ethical situation or transgression. Managers need to know not only who was involved and what happened but also the when, why, where, and how. These facts and data will help managers to perform the steps for addressing the intensity of the response (soon to be discussed). Just as importantly, they will help them to perform the next step.

Five, determine whether to personally address the ethical issue or transgression or seek outside help. The fact is that managers can go only so far in what they can do without dissipating their energies in managing their project or getting themselves embroiled in a legal situation. For simple, minor ethical situations or transgressions, their involvement may be okay; however, for those that may have severe impacts, they may need to bring in their management or make other contacts. It is not advisable to become a self-appointed attorney or what was called in the army a "latrine lawyer."

Six, assuming managers can handle the issue or transgression, they should have at this point a good idea as to the cause or causes. Knowing the cause or causes helps in determining the appropriate solution. Without knowing the cause or causes, they may never really address the ethical issue or transgression. For example, they may think they have addressed it, but other stakeholders know that the ethical issue or transgression still remains. Failure to address the cause will communicate to others only that they have—whether true—a tolerance for unethical decisions or actions. It is a bad precedent to set.

2.8 INTENSITY OF RESPONSE

For intensity of response, here are the steps, assuming project managers are managing the dilemma themselves:

One, meet with the stakeholders who are involved in the ethical situation or transgression. These are the stakeholders who caused it to happen and the ones who are impacted by it. They can be met with individually or as a group. Ideally, they should start talking about how to resolve any misunderstandings and eventually to come up with a solution that addresses the causes and, of course, that everyone can live with. If this action is taken unilaterally, the project manager will be in a position of a police officer enforcing his own solution on others who, quite simply, do not like it. Of course, one of the solutions may be to not do anything but instead communicate it up to management or some other route such as a hotline.

Two, assuming everyone agrees to the solution they developed, the goal is for them to participate in developing a plan that not only will rectify what has occurred but also will ensure that it will not happen again. The formality of the plan depends, of course, on the sensitivity of the issue or transgression and the degree to which everyone wants to avoid facing the same circumstances again. Judgment is critical here because a plan in which the cost exceeds the benefits is not desired. Above all, the plan demonstrates that the managers are preparing to resolve the ethical situation or transgression. The managers are demonstrating due diligence.

Three, implement the plan that everyone hopefully has reached consensus over. The extent to which the plan is implemented will be directly correlated with its effectiveness. Ideally, the plan is simple enough to implement and may require a simple schedule and a periodic review. A status report from key stakeholders should give an idea as to whether the plan was implemented. Implementing a plan, albeit even a simple one, communicates to everyone that the entire endeavor is more than just going through the motions. The project manager and others are committed and serious. Most importantly, this step demonstrates due care.

Four, tied closely to the last step, project managers must follow up on the effectiveness of the solution and the plan implementing it. In this way they are demonstrating to others the importance of the issue and transgression and its solution. They are also helping to continue focus on completing the project, not constantly acting as the project's police officer. The effectiveness can often be determined as the plan is implemented. Perhaps, however, the two most important follow-up actions that can be done are to determine if corrective action is necessary and to implement and conduct a "lessons learned" session, which can help in avoiding similar ethical situations and transgressions and how to effectively deal with similar ones in the future.

2.9 FINAL THOUGHTS

Project managers are unique in a sense that they are the only ones who function as a hub among all the stakeholders on their projects. They are also the only ones who are postured to see the "big picture"; most others have a partial perspective. Coupled with being a hub and having a big picture perspective is often having little or no formal power and authority to deal with hard and soft technical issues. Yet when such issues arise, project managers can find their projects, their organizations, and themselves in trouble unless they have a model facing ethical dilemmas.

2.10 GETTING STARTED CHECKLIST

Question	Yes	No
1. When thinking about ethics, have you considered the unique circumstances that you confront as a project manager when dealing with ethical situations?		
Being surrounded by people with a narrow disciplinary focus		
Working with different stakeholders		
Having responsibility without commensurate authority		
Receiving pressure to achieve results in a relatively short period of time		
Making short-term decisions that could have long-term consequences		
Having temporary work relationships		
Working in different environments		
General business environment over which you have no control		
2. On your project, will you be addressing "hard" ethical issues like the following?		
Legal compliance		
Due diligence and due care		
Employment at will		
Employee rights		
Employee health and safety		
Contracts and agreements		
Bribes and kickbacks		
Conflicts of interest		

Question	Yes	No
Mischarging		
Padding and low-balling		
Insider trading		
Quality		
Reporting		
Unfair competitive advantage		
3. On your project, will you be addressing "soft" ethical issues like the following?		
Short- and long-term perspectives		
Commitment, responsibility, and accountability		
Culture		
Behavior		
Motivation		
Pressure		
Setting priorities		
Communication		
4. If you face an ethical situation and fail to act, have you considered the impact of consequences like the following on yourself, your project, and the overall organization?		
Tarnished reputation		
Tarnished credibility		
Litigation		
5. When dealing with ethical situations, have you considered the wide range of influences that could affect your objectivity, such as the following?		
Being a product of your background		
Difficulty in releasing yourself from your time and place		
Knowing when you have enough facts and data about the issue		
Understanding your frame of reference		
4. When facing an ethical dilemma, do you consider the following consequences of your decision and actions?		
Positive (decision)		

Continued

Question		Yes	No
	Negative (decision)		
	Positive (action)		
	Negative (action)		
5.	When determining sensitivity of an ethical issue, do you consider the following?		
	Magnitude		
	Scalability		
	Context		
	Ramifications of acting or not acting		
	Your degree of control over the situation related to the ethical issue		
	Appropriate amount of facts and data		
	Impact to stakeholders		
	Consequences of your assessment		
	Reliability of assumptions		
	Causes		
	Degree of impact to the response		
6.	Do you consider the following steps for addressing the sensitivity of an ethical issue?		
	Determining if an ethical issue has arisen		
	Assuming an ethical issue, determining its sensitivity		
	Identifying stakeholders involved in an ethical situation or transgression		
	Conducting an inquiry to collect the relevant facts and data related to the ethical issue		
	Determining whether to address the ethical issue yourself or seek outside help		
	Assuming you can handle the issue, formulating a good idea as to the issue's cause or causes		
7.	Do you consider the following steps for addressing the intensity of response to an ethical issue?		
	Meeting with stakeholders who are involved in the ethical issue		

Question	Yes	No
Assuming everyone agrees to a solution they developed, encouraging them to participate in developing a plan that will not only rectify what has occurred but also ensure that it will not happen again		
Implementing the plan for which everyone has reached consensus		
Following up on the effectiveness of the solution and the plan for implementing it		

3

Project Management Code of Ethics

Just about all professions have a code of ethics, and project management is no exception. Thanks to organizations like the Project Management Institute© (PMI), a code of ethics exists.

In their book *Professional Liability and Risk Management*, Bruce Bennett et al. identified the structure of an ethical framework embodied in a code of ethics. They noted that there is an overall system of principles that provides structure for a code of ethics. This structure, in turn, is built on a set of principles that comprise the system of ethics. The principles allow the development of standards found acceptable to authorities and general practices in the field. These standards are followed by guidelines, which are really procedures to apply as standards in the field.[*]

3.1 BENEFITS

A code of ethics offers many benefits:

One, it provides a structure that all people in the profession can use to make decisions. Today, typical professions exist around the globe. Laws and customs as well as how they respond to ethical situations vary. An ethical framework works, as long as it is accepted by all or most members of a profession, as a means of getting people to operate according to some common principles regardless of where they are on the planet.

---

[*] Bruce Bennett, Brenda Bryant, Gary VandenBos, and Addison Greenwood, *Professional Liability and Risk Management* (Washington, DC: American Psychological Association, 1990), pp. 17–18.

Two, because it provides a common structure for a profession, it offers the potential for a common language from a disciplinary standpoint. Whether one speaks Chinese, Swahili, English, or Yiddish, the terms used in the code of ethics have a similar meaning, albeit with differences in interpretation. All nationalities at least have vocabulary that is considered acceptable at a certain level of abstraction.

Three, it provides a way to deal with ethical situations that are grayer rather than black and white. Situations arise that are not always clear and that require judgment. A code of ethics provides help in making decisions and taking the right action under such circumstances. While logic and intuition are helpful, a professional sometimes faces situations that require the use of a code of ethics to help provide direction.

Four, it provides a sense of community among people in a discipline. Regardless of location or ethnicity, a code of ethics serves as a way to bridge the gap among them. They adhere to the same principles, to the same tools and techniques, and to a common vocabulary. It may seem to create a camaraderie or esprit de corps among the members of the profession.

Five, it provides guidelines for disciplining members of the profession who fail to adhere to the contents of the code. The principles, standards, and guidelines offer a way to determine what is acceptable and not acceptable according to the code. Transgressions of the code lay the groundwork for removing people who fail to live up to its creed.

Six, it keeps the profession alive, meaning that it furthers and encourages dialogue over issues and circumstances that would ordinarily lose visibility among the members of the community. Conferences and publications help to provide that visibility through the discussions of issues and circumstances, especially those dealing with ethics, in the forefront of people's minds. This benefit encourages greater dialogue and sharing of insights, which contributes to the knowledge base of the entire discipline.

Finally, it enables the transfer of principles and knowledge from one generation of members of a discipline to the next. It provides continuity in dealing with issues and circumstances in a way that capitalizes on acceptable standards and guidelines. In other words, each generation of a discipline does not have to reinvent everything, leading to meaningless trial and error and sometimes needless frustration and misery. Instead, each succeeding generation can benefit from the principles of the previous one when dealing with ethical issues and circumstances.

3.2 DOWNSIDES

Of course, as with anything, with benefits come some downsides, and a code of ethics is no different.

One, it can foster rigidity of thought if the code is inflexible. Tools, concepts, and practices that vary from the principles may be condemned by the professional organization, which may lead to an increase in knowledge of the profession or to valuable people leaving the profession to apply new tools, concepts, and practices due to the intolerance of the current membership.

Two, it may cause some members to interpret principles as simply as the "law" and, consequently, to suspend judgment. This lack of judgment can cause a lack of feeling on the part of the professional for any sense of responsibility for the results. In other words, professionals simply absolve themselves from any consequences because they were simply following the code of ethics. Or worse, it may serve as an excuse to do something that may, ironically, appear unethical.

Lastly, it contains principles and terminology that are often so vague that they can be used to justify anything. Professionals in the field can cite a passage or term that, depending on its interpretation, provides justification for their decisions or actions dealing with an ethical issue or circumstance.

Essentially, a code of ethics is simply a way to provide professionals with a set of principles, standards, and guidelines for dealing with ethical issues and circumstances. It does not replace judgment either on an individual or group level. It does not offer excuses for making decisions and taking actions that harm individuals and threatens the overall public good. In other words, it requires that professionals take a sense of personal responsibility for decisions and actions while using it as a framework to exercise judgment.

3.3 CATEGORIES OF PRINCIPLES

As a separate system of principles, project management is a relatively new phenomenon, at least in the United States, although in the past it was often mixed in with other professions, such as engineering or medicine. The

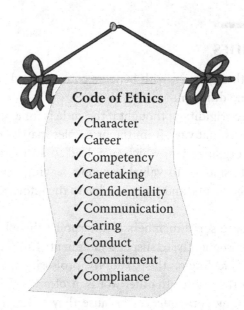

FIGURE 3.1
Typical contents for a code of ethics.

ethical principles that support some of the existing codes of ethics in project management can be categorized into 10 groups, as outlined in this section. These categories are not mutually exclusive as you might suspect; they overlap with each other, and failure of one may and often does infect one or more of the others. While there is no particular order to them, notice that character is at the top of the list. There is a good reason for this (Figure 3.1):

1. Character
2. Career
3. Competency
4. Caretaking
5. Confidentiality
6. Communication
7. Caring
8. Conduct
9. Commitment
10. Compliance

3.3.1 Character

This one matters a lot, yet unfortunately it often seems to go to the wayside for all sorts of reasons discussed in this book. Character traits like courage, honesty, judgment, and sense of right or wrong seem no longer relevant until an ethical situation or transgression arises. While such terms are vague and open to interpretation, the reality is that when they fail to be exercised on a project they become quite apparent. For example, a project manager who lacks courage will often be a weak project manager by not addressing issues that should have been addressed. Naturally, these issues will lead to problems sometime later during the product or project life cycle. The same can be said for honesty; a project manager who fails to be honest will lose credibility with stakeholders.

A failure in character will affect all the other ethical categories described in the forthcoming paragraphs. It will permeate everything like tainted blood corrupting all the organs of the body. For example, dishonesty may make it difficult for project managers to share their knowledge; reduce their credibility in communicating with stakeholders; lead them to wonder whether leadership truly cares about the project; or, trust their competency.

    A. Standard: Take the high road at all times.
    B. Standard: Be consistent in thought and action.
    C. Standard: Exhibit moral as well as physical courage.

Project managers will always have to face a test of character. There will be circumstances which will present what seem to be overwhelming odds if you follow your own ethical principles or those of your profession. There will also be circumstances which will not be so obvious a challenge; they may be so subtle that you may not realize it until after the fact. The best that project managers can do is ingrain the principles of the profession with those of their own to make the best possible judgment.

3.3.2 Career

Project managers have basically three ways to enhance their career: one oriented toward themselves and the other two toward their profession:

- Standard: Keep knowledge and expertise up to contemporary standards, not just for personal reasons but also for the people or organizations to which services are provided. Actions include taking training and seminars on the latest topics affecting the profession; reading articles and books related to these and other topics; and increasing knowledge and experience of application of concepts, principles, techniques, and tools.
- Standard: Participate in professional societies or associations related to project management. This participation includes sharing knowledge and experiences with colleagues via presentations and papers at local chapter meetings and conventions; further imparting background information through seminars and workshops; holding leadership positions within the societies; and keeping abreast of the latest principles, standards, and guidelines of the organization.
- Standard: Become and stay a member of good standing with the society or association, which means following the principles of the organization; embodying behavior with these principles in the organization and the public; not engaging in activities that use the organization for material gain or illegal behavior; not lying about or exaggerating knowledge and experience in the field; and not accepting positions, based on falsehoods, that clearly go beyond knowledge and expertise (unless, of course, those who employ the managers' services are aware of their shortcomings in this regard).

Project managers should be active participants in their profession. Failure to get involved hurts themselves and the profession because they have experiences and knowledge. They can do so by publishing articles and books; teaching at local universities and colleges, and serving as officers in local chapters of project management societies.

3.3.3 Competency

Closely related to career is competency—that is, having the knowledge and experience to work in the field of project management. Being competent in project management, like most professions, requires practical experience; book learning is not enough. There are ways for project managers to demonstrate their competency.

- Standard: Demonstrate due diligence and due care by applying and following the processes advocated by the professional societies in project management. In other words, project managers should use their judgment when applying project management concepts, principles, tools, and techniques. Knowing the project life cycle is not enough; applying project management knowledge to it is what matters, and this can come only from experience. For example, project managers should always have a charter, work breakdown structure, and schedule for a project; otherwise they are being unethical by not doing what is expected of them as professionals.
- Standard: Avoid taking shortcuts that will have a short-term fix but severe long-term consequences to be addressed by someone else. This especially has ethical consequences if project managers fail to communicate these consequences to the customer. Of course, managers cannot be clairvoyants, but it is unethical to know about these consequences and to tell no one.
- Standard: Accept responsibility for defects and errors on personal projects. Project managers—and no one else—are responsible for the overall results of their team. Blaming someone else (which is not the same as identifying the source of a problem) is shirking responsibility. A key point is that managers can delegate work, but they cannot do the same with responsibility. Trying to do so will only demonstrate unwillingness to take ownership.
- Standard: Apply the latest developments in the field of project management; challenge others to do so as well. Always adhering to past ways of doing business may actually lead to ineffective and inefficient execution of a project. New tools and techniques are constantly being designed; if they are applicable to the project and can enhance its planning and execution, their application needs to be considered. This will enhance not only the progress of the project but also the perception of the project manager's competence.

Project managers will always face challenges and opportunities for displaying competency in their profession. Many project managers lack formal control over the resources to complete their projects. They must use a combination of hard (e.g., scheduling) and soft (e.g., negotiation) skills to bring their projects to a successful conclusion. To do so requires individuals who not only have theoretical knowledge but also practical experience; the combination of the two will enable them to exhibit a competency commensurate with their background for dealing with ethical dilemmas and making the right decisions for their projects.

3.3.4 Caretaking

Project managers are given a huge responsibility: They must harness the resources given to them by their management and execute projects that will achieve the goals and objectives not only of the projects but also of the overall organization. This responsibility covers labor (e.g., people) and nonlabor (e.g., equipment) resources. Caretaking requires project managers to take several actions:

- Standard: Do not use company resources for managers' purposes. For example, they should not use a resource entrusted to them to add value to their own personal resources. They must use the resources to further the gains of the project; to do otherwise is a violation of trust. Often, people assume that this principle applies only to people in public service, but that is not the case. The principle applies to project managers of private or public organizations, too. Shareholders and other stakeholders have hired them to apply resources to complete a project successfully, not to line their coffers with the resources of the project in some way.
- Standard: Employ resources effectively and efficiently. Effectiveness means achieving the goals and objectives of the project; efficiency is achieving the goals and objectives in ways that deliver the desired level of quality for the least cost. Experienced project managers know that a balance exists between the two; that is, equilibrium exists between both. The most expensive and cheapest approaches are not necessarily the best ones and do not necessarily translate into success. Project managers must seek to complete their project in a way that delivers the most value for the money expended.
- Standard: Focus on the greater good. Sometimes this goes beyond the project itself. A project is often part of a much bigger initiative or program of a company, especially large ones. Project managers must take a big picture perspective and then make a decision. Sometimes

that perspective can put them at odds with some stakeholders on their project. Their perspective may even go beyond that of their company to consider the public's interest. What may appear good for a project and the parent organization, such as a financial perspective, may actually hurt the life, safety, health, and overall welfare of the public. Under such scenarios, project managers will have to make a hard decision over which to choose. The right decision is to put the public welfare above all others, yet such decisions are often not easy to make.

- Standard: Keep the needs and wants of the customers at the forefront, whether confronted with black-and-white or gray issues. After all, customers are likely paying for project managers' knowledge and services and for those of the entire project. If those interests are unclear or have changed, it is incumbent upon the project manager to work with other project managers to steer the project in the direction of meeting their requirements.
- Standard: Ensure that if partners or customers provide resources, such as products or designs, they have secured the right to use them in the development and delivery of a product or service. In other words, they should not use resources that do not belong to them unless given the expressed permission to do so. Using material without permission from the owner is theft.
- Standard: Be willing to acknowledge if a mistake is made, and take the necessary action to correct it. For example, if a project manager made a mistake in employing resources, she should acknowledge it even in front of the customer, if necessary, and take appropriate action to resolve the problem. Such action will demonstrate that you take their investment in you and your project seriously and that you can be trusted to take corrective action whenever the circumstances involving the use of resources go awry.

Caring for project resources is not easy. These resources can take many forms. The tangible resources (e.g., equipment) are often easier to take care of because they can be tagged or essentially secured in a restricted area. Resources such as data and intellectual property are harder to keep track of and secure; once projects lose control of them it is harder, if not impossible, to recover them.

3.3.5 Confidentiality

This one is closely allied with caretaking, except it is more involved with not revealing information entrusted to the project managers and members of their team. Project managers are quite often responsible for protecting and using data and personally identifiable information (PII) discreetly on their projects. For example, they may be building a strategic business system that contains critical information about the direction of a company. They may be working with a business partner who is sharing sensitive information that cannot be released outside the purview of a project. Whatever the reason, managers have been entrusted with vital data and information that requires control. Failure to do so can result in severe consequences to the organization, the project, and the manager. Here are some general principles concerning the confidentiality of information on a project:

- Standard: Do not use proprietary information for personal gain. A perfect example is insider trading, where a project manager uses highly proprietary information that will have an eventual impact on the value of stock; having such information will give the manager an unfair competitive advantage vis-à-vis other investors.
- Standard: Be judicious in handling sensitive data and information. Project managers who possess restricted data or information that is not to be released are responsible for taking the necessary precautions to maintain that confidentiality. Failure to restrict access to that information represents carelessness and a breach of confidence.
- Standard: Establish controls to restrict access and release of sensitive information. Project managers are responsible for the overall performance of their project. An important aspect, of course, is ensuring that the resources including sensitive data and information are managed with the utmost care. Controls should be instituted to minimize the probability and impact should they become compromised.
- Standard: Do not use sensitive data and information that should not have been revealed in the first place. If project managers receive data and information that could result in a legal violation, such as data and information that give the company an unfair competitive advantage, appropriate action must be taken immediately. Using such data or information to win a contract imperils the project manager and the organization legally.

3.3.6 Communication

This one is an important responsibility of a project manager. As mentioned earlier, project managers communicate 90 percent of their time with other stakeholders, whether vertically (i.e., up and down the chain of command) or horizontally (i.e., with peers). Ethically, some actions to take or avoid when communicating with stakeholders are:

- Standard: Present information objectively and truthfully. Project managers, if for no other reason than to establish and maintain credibility, should communicate in a way that people will rely on what they convey. In other words, they do not "massage" data and information to achieve some ulterior motive; their communications should be balanced, giving a true picture, for instance, about the state of a project. This means presenting data and information that may not look good for themselves or other key stakeholders on a project, which is not an easy thing to do and, not surprisingly, is rarely done. It takes considerable courage to present such messages.
- Standard: Don't distort or alter facts and data. Seek and communicate truthfully. Project managers need to tell all the important facts and data regarding a topic so that the right decision can be made by the right people. To do otherwise is risking credibility not just with the facts and data but with the individuals communicating them. Consequences, positive and negative, need to be communicated.
- Standard: Be direct without being blunt. Project managers should be willing to state what the fundamental issue is concerning a negative circumstance and not couch it with excuses, needless explanations, or blame toward someone or something. They should state what they think are the causes, triggers, and impacts and must be willing to deal with conflict in the same way; failure to be direct about a conflict only causes it to increase in intensity and makes it more complicated to deal with later in the project life cycle.
- Standard: Establish and maintain an environment for open communications. Project managers should not allow, for example, groupthink or a shoot the messenger mentality to prevail. When open communications fail to exist, data and information get distorted, leading to erroneous decisions and actions by key stakeholders. An uninhibited atmosphere is critical to ensuring that open communications exist.

- Standard: Be willing to receive as well as to give criticism. This one is not easy because it requires an element of self-effacement and tolerance. However, receiving and delivering criticism allows project managers to grow and adapt effectively to the environment. The problem is often not the criticism but how it is delivered and received; taken from a positive perspective, it becomes a gift.
- Standard: Be an individual. Project managers need to communicate in a manner that does not require people to question whether there is a hidden motive behind what is being said. If people think or even perceive that the project managers are simply instruments for someone or are being influenced by some interested party, they will not trust what is being communicated and credibility will be lost.

3.3.7 Caring

Expressing a genuine concern for stakeholders on projects is an ethical responsibility of project managers. It centers on treating others with respect by recognizing their differences while at the same time getting them to work together to achieve a common goal. A stereotypical view of people is not only an outdated style of project management but also can cause ethical issues to arise. For example, people may begin treating others in a way that does not respect their cultural or religious differences, resulting not only in poor performance but also in legal complications.

Project managers can demonstrate caring from an ethical standpoint in several ways:

- Standard: Embrace diversity. In today's global environment, projects can involve several different cultures and countries, with people spanning many religions, races, and nationalities. However, diversity goes beyond these characteristics. It also involves embracing diversity from a thinking standpoint. Increasingly, project managers and other stakeholders are recognizing that diversity also involves people viewing the world differently simply because of the way that they think using mental models. These models help people to make sense of the world, determining what data and information are important and what actions to take to respond to what they know. Project managers, therefore, require good effective listening and empathy skills to motivate people to achieve the goals and objectives of their projects.

- Standard: Avoid embracing ethnocentrism—that is, the view that one culture is superior to that of other cultures or nationalities. In a world of globalization, of course, such an attitude is folly because it can prove divisive to project teams and alienate stakeholders. The opposite of ethnocentrism is polycentrism, recognizing that no one culture is superior to the other or that the world centers on just one.
- Standard: Don't discriminate. Discrimination comes in many forms, not just race or sex. It can be due to mental models, for example. Some project managers like to surround themselves with people who think and behave like them. The danger is that when project managers find themselves surrounded by mirror images of themselves they might not recognize or admit that ethical dilemmas exist. Groupthink might take over, causing people to screen any indicators that an ethical issue or transgression exists.
- Standard: Provide opportunities for everyone, not just for a few. If they become selective, project managers find that they have encapsulated themselves with clones, so to speak, and provide most of the opportunities to them. The ones who are excluded (and are probably upset about it) may find ways to show vengeance by behaving in a way that could cause ethical dilemmas to arise. For example, they may exhibit behavior that violates the rights of colleagues or sabotages the project in some way.
- Standard: Create and maintain a positive working environment. Thus, stakeholders will be more likely to identify or uncover ethical issues and violations without fear of reprisal. They will also be willing to share ideas on how to address ethical issues and violations. To make such an environment a reality, project managers must adopt a view similar to Douglas McGregor's Theory Y rather than Theory X. Project managers who subscribe to Theory Y view people positively: self-motivated, enjoying working, and able to operate with minimal supervision. Project managers who subscribe to Theory X take a different view of people and see them as lazy, not to be trusted, and requiring close supervision. As you might suspect, people working under project managers adhering to Theory Y will be likely to disclose ethical issues and violations rather than try to cover them up.[*]

---

[*] Rita Mulcahy, PMP Exam Prep, 6th ed. (Minnetonka, MN: RMC Publications, 2009), 333.

- Standard: Treat all people with respect. In other words, don't act abusively by taking Theory X to the extreme. Demeaning individuals in front of team members, ignoring recognition when a person exceeds expectations, and deliberately not keeping certain individuals informed of specific information can become abusive if carried to the extreme, in which case it becomes harassment.
- Standard: Give credit to stakeholders who deserve it, and never personally take credit when it should be shared with others. If someone makes a significant contribution on the project team, project managers should ensure that the right individual gets the accolades. Failure to do so can build resentment and lead to one or more persons seeking retaliation through unethical means simply to get even.
- Standard: Provide a safe environment, both physically and psychologically. Physical safety means that people should be able to perform their tasks in an environment free from physical harm. Psychological safety means ensuring that people are treated with respect without fear of being harassed or ridiculed by other stakeholders. If some individuals feel that their physical or psychological safety is threatened, they will do whatever they have to protect themselves, even if it means doing something unethical.
- Standard: Be willing to assist other team members when they need help. This action demonstrates care for others and for their success. When project managers help others to succeed, the favor is almost always returned. If, on the other hand, managers simply bark orders and offer no help for whatever reason, the team members may think their manager does not care and, in return, may do something unethical without caring what the consequences are.
- Standard: Be self-aware. Are the appropriate messages being sent to stakeholders, especially team members? Body language communicates attitude. Taken to the extreme, people on the receiving end may view a negative attitude as an excuse to do something unethical because the message being sent was one of "I don't care." If the project manager does not care, after all, why should they?
- Standard: Listen. When working with stakeholders, apply active and effective listening. Not only does this action show that managers care, but, when dealing with an ethical issue or transgression, it helps them uncover its source and may even reveal ideas for how to deal with it. Not listening may result in overlooking key facts or data about an ethical situation and transgression or taking the wrong approach to resolve it.

When project managers demonstrate that they care about others on the team, it pays ethical rewards. It shows that team members are being taken seriously and are seen as valued members of the project and that their manager's fate is tied directly to them. It increases the odds that people will take the high road.

3.3.8 Conduct

This one occurs on two levels—the project manager's and others. Managers' thoughts and behavior reveal much about their character; others will feed off their thoughts and behavior, which can make a difference between doing what is right and what is wrong. The thoughts and actions of others can reveal much about them, too. It is important, therefore, that project managers' thoughts and actions demonstrate taking the high road throughout the life of a project. Here are some important things to keep in mind regarding conduct:

- Standard: Be fair in all dealings. Project managers and every stakeholder should be willing to listen to each other whenever an ethical dilemma arises. Coming to a conclusion before hearing all the facts and data can only hinder resolution since those involved may feel slighted in some way. The ethical dilemma can then escalate in visibility and magnitude.
- Standard: Be independent and objective by not accepting bribes, kickbacks, or other illegal favors. While this might sound like common sense, the news reports of scandals in major corporations indicate such unethical behavior is prevalent at all levels of hierarchy.
- Standard: Don't get into a situation in which there is an actual or perceived conflict of interest. If this happens, alert the proper people and seek guidance on altering the level and degree of involvement.
- Standard: Negotiate in good faith. Negotiation can occur internally with other functional managers or externally with vendors. Not negotiating in good faith should not be tolerated because people could end up feeling or being misled or misrepresented, causing suspicions to arise. People who feel that a project manager did not negotiate in good faith may retaliate by doing something unethical.
- Standard: Accept responsibility for decisions, actions, and results. Everyone on a project should accept ownership for their respective parts. Ownership makes good sense. People will feel more

emotionally committed to achieve a positive result. Just as importantly, they will likely be more inclined not to engage in unethical
behavior because they will want to be successful. Of course, they can
take ownership to the extreme and conduct themselves unethically
to complete a project successfully; naturally, such behavior should be
discouraged. The end does not justify the means.

- Standard: Do not compromise ethics because of pressure. Sometimes
the rewards of a project or the fear of penalty can lead some people to
exhibit unethical conduct that they would not under ordinary circumstances. All stakeholders must guard against the tendency to succumb
to pressure from someone with more power, as Stanley Milgram so
aptly demonstrated. The Stanley Milgram experiment demonstrated
that people have a desie to obey a person of authority, even when it
meant violating their conscience. *

Conduct is closely interwoven with character. Individuals with strong
character will likely not conduct themselves in an unethical manner.
Yet sometimes without even realizing it they may find themselves doing
just that. Time and circumstances can coalesce, which may contribute
to a decision on an ethical dilemma and have unethical results.*

3.3.9 Commitment

Dedication is another word for commitment. People commit themselves
to their projects. They want the project to succeed, which means they
commit their time, energies, skills, and knowledge to achieve a successful
outcome as defined by key stakeholders. Here are some ways to exhibit
commitment to the success of a project:

- Standard: Walk the talk. Project managers should not only say they
are committed to the project, but they should also demonstrate it
through word and deed. That may mean fighting to resolve a serious issue despite the negative impact to them personally, working
diligently to procure the resources that they promised, working long
hours side by side with the team as they struggle to meet a major
milestone even though it may be unnecessary, or taking the high

---

* Gregory Berns, Iconoclast: A Neuroscientist Reveals How to Think Differently (Boston: Harvard
Business Press, 2008), 132-135.

road even at potential expense to their career. If managers fail to walk the talk, some stakeholders will not take what the managers do or say seriously and could do something unethical as a result.

- Standard: Follow through on promises; otherwise, expectations will be dashed. Promising something that cannot be delivered can lead to frustration and anger, with which comes the potential for people to do something unethical in ways that can result in embarrassment to the project manager, the project, and the organization.
- Standard: Set the tone. Project managers should let stakeholders know that they embrace the high road when managing the project. It is okay to ask if something is the right thing to do. So often during the course of a project people become so busy working that no one takes time to ask that simple question. For example, individual or group behavior becomes so intense that people may not even realize the ethical consequences of their work.
- Standard: Do not compete against the employer in a side business. No one can be expected to provide a service or product to a customer if he or she is already providing that same one during full-time employment—for example, providing the same service to an employer's customer but at a cheaper price in an after-hours personal consulting business.

3.3.10 Compliance

All stakeholders need to follow the laws, regulations, policies, and procedures that govern the project. Failure to comply can put a company, not just a project, at financial, legal, and reputational risk. What follows are some behaviors and actions to adhere to regarding compliance:

- Standard: Obey copyright, patent, and trademark laws. While some people and organizations may get away with violating them, others may get caught, and the penalties—from financial to reputational—are severe. When in doubt, consult with legal professionals.
- Standard: Support disclosure when discovering noncompliance. Trying to hide the evidence can be just as damaging as the ethical violation itself. Many times noncompliance is due to ignorance or mistakes and less frequently to intent. Stakeholders should feel comfortable bringing up and openly discussing ethical or other issues resulting from noncompliance. If not, a problem exists.

- Standard: Apply laws, regulations, policies, and procedures consistently and fairly. Being selective in their application can lead to claims of exhibiting favoritism and even discrimination. Everyone needs to comply with applicable laws, regulations, policies, and procedures, and these same ones need to apply to everyone equally, except in extreme mitigating circumstances—and then under close scrutiny.
- Standard: Cooperate with investigators and auditors. If an ethical compliance issue is being investigated, project managers and all stakeholders need to cooperate fully. If a project manager holds back essential information, it is an ethical failure because she is condoning the behavior and may even be construed as protecting individuals who were noncompliant. Even if an issue is not readily apparent, project managers should cooperate; failure to do so puts not only them but also other stakeholders and the overall organization or company at risk.

3.4 FINAL THOUGHTS

Codes of ethics are important to a profession, but they are meaningless if they are simply platitudes that no one follows. They can be viewed as something to strive for, but they are much more. They also provide guidance on executing responsibilities and resolving ethical dilemmas. Failure to apply codes perhaps remains nothing more than a hope, even a dream.

3.5 GETTING STARTED CHECKLIST

	Question	Yes	No
1.	Does your company's or profession's code of ethics offer the following benefits?		
	A structure that all people can use to make decisions		
	A common language		
	A way to deal with ethical issues that are grayer than black and white		
	A sense of community among all its members		

Question		Yes	No
	Guidelines for disciplining members who fail to adhere to the contents of the code		
	Dialogue over issues and circumstances that would ordinarily lose visibility among the members of the community		
	Transfer of principles and knowledge from one generation of members to the next		
2.	Does your company's or profession's code of ethics have the following downsides?		
	Rigidity of thought		
	Interpretation of principles as law		
	Vague terminology		
3.	Does your code of ethics address the following principles?		
	Character		
	Career		
	Competency		
	Caretaking		
	Confidentiality		
	Communication		
	Caring		
	Conduct		
	Commitment		
	Compliance		
4.	For the principle of character, do you adhere to the following standards?		
	Take the high road at all times		
	Be consistent in thought and action		
	Exhibit moral as well as physical courage		
5.	For the principle of career, do you adhere to the following standards?		
	Keep up your knowledge and expertise to contemporary standards		
	Participate in professional societies or associations related to project management		
	Become and stay a member of good standing with the society or association		

Continued

Question		Yes	No
6.	For the principle of competency, do you adhere to the following standards?		
	Demonstrate due diligence and due care by applying and following the processes advocated by professional societies		
	Avoid taking shortcuts you know will have a short-term fix but have severe long-term consequences that will have to be addressed by someone else		
	Accept responsibility for defects and errors if they occur on your project		
	Challenge yourself and others to apply the latest developments in the field of project management		
7.	For the principle of caretaking, do you adhere to the following standards?		
	Not use company resources for own purposes		
	Employ resources effectively and efficiently		
	Focus on the greater good		
	Keep the needs and wants of the customer in the forefront of stakeholders' minds		
	Ensure that if a partner or customer provides resources that they have secured the right to use them in the development and delivery of a product or service		
8.	For the principle of confidentiality, do you adhere to the following standards?		
	Do not use proprietary information for your own personal gain		
	Be judicious in handling sensitive data and information		
	Establish controls to restrict access and release of sensitive information		
	Do not use sensitive data and information that you should not have in the first place		
9.	For the principle of communication, do you adhere to the following standards?		
	Present information objectively and truthfully		
	Not distort or alter facts and data		
	Be direct in communicating without being blunt		

Question		Yes	No
	Establish and maintain an environment for open communications		
	Be willing to receive as well as give criticism		
	Be an individual		
10.	For the principle of caring, do you adhere to the following standards?		
	Embrace diversity		
	Avoid ethnocentrism		
	Do not discriminate		
	Provide opportunities for everyone		
	Create and maintain a positive working environment		
	Treat all people with respect		
	Give credit to stakeholders who deserve it and by no means take credit for anything for yourself when it should be shared with others		
	Be willing to assist other team members when they need help		
	Be aware of your behavior		
	Listen		
11.	For the principle of conduct, do you adhere to the following standards?		
	Be fair in all dealings		
	Be independent and objective by not accepting bribes, kickbacks, or other illegal favors		
	Avoid conflicts of interest		
	Negotiate in good faith		
	Accept responsibility for decisions, actions, and results		
	Do not compromise ethics because of pressure		
12.	For the principle of commitment, do you adhere to the following standards?		
	Walk the talk		
	Follow through on your promises		
	Set the tone		
	Do not compete against your employer in a side business		

Continued

Question		Yes	No
13.	For the principle of compliance, do you adhere to the following standards?		
	Obey copyright, patent, and trademark laws		
	Support disclosure when discovering noncompliance		
	Apply laws, regulations, policies, and procedures consistently and fairly		
	Cooperate with investigators and auditors		

4

The Ethical Trends and Challenges Confronting Project Managers

Before discussing some of the specific challenges that can cause stakeholders on a project to face ethical dilemmas, this chapter addresses some of the trends that precipitate them. The potential ethical issues that these trends present can have considerable implications for projects, organizations, and individuals, so it is important to recognize them.

4.1 GLOBAL TRENDS

1. *Greater globalization*: Over the last 30 to 40 years, international commerce has grown so dramatically that projects involving people from different cultures have become the norm rather than the exception. This has presented some challenges from an ethical perspective. Different customs, ways of doing business, laws, and governmental regulations have added to the already complex world of project management. Couple all that with language differences, politics, and history, and it is no surprise that the likelihood is high on these projects that stakeholders will face some sort of ethical situation or transgression.

2. *Importance of intellectual property* (IP): Intellectual property is influencing projects to a greater degree than ever before. With the growth in knowledge as a means of production comes the need to protect knowledge to acquire and maintain competitive advantage. This trend will increase with the corresponding growth in information technology (IT) as a key way to seize market advantage. In today's

work environment, projects involve many different disciplines in various industries, with each specialty playing a critical role in success or failure. IP plays a crucial role in protecting the output of those specialties, which increases the chance of project managers ending up in ethical dilemmas due to the rise of a knowledge-based economy, the role of partnerships, and an increasingly competitive environment.

3. *More rights in the workplace*: Although the laws still lean in favor of the employer, employees are increasingly finding that their rights are becoming more important than ever. A web of laws and regulations from different governmental jurisdictions has afforded various legal protections of employees, ranging from using computing technology to hiring practices for people of different ethnicities. These legal measures have permeated all aspects of business, including the project environment. Projects managers and other key stakeholders now need greater awareness of these measures because whatever action they take in response to an ethical dilemmas can have legal implications for their company and themselves.

4. *Greater regulatory oversight*: Government is increasingly regulating the affairs of business. The relationships among all the entities and systems have become more complex, with which comes the opportunity for something to go awry due to terrorism, corruption, or political instability. Governments, whether by choice or force, will get more and more involved in the affairs of businesses, especially on projects. For instance, many trade laws apply to projects that preclude the export of information or technology to other countries. Other laws deal with the relations with certain categories of people. Project managers can easily find themselves in serious ethical situations and transgressions without realizing it and will end up facing fines and penalties not just for their companies but also for themselves, not to mention potential imprisonment and embarrassment.

5. *Outsourcing*: This business practice in the business environment morphs from one form of business arrangement to another (e.g., co-sourcing, near sourcing). Outsourcing has been increasing, and will continue to do so, as businesses seek ways to lower their costs and escape regulations. Outsourcing, of course, can occur both domestically and internationally (e.g., offset agreements), and although it may raise revenues and avoid regulatory behavior, it also builds

resentment among individuals who have been and could possibility be victims of it. With this resentment comes the possibility of people committing ethical transgressions as a way to seek vengeance for what is perceived as an uncaring, disloyal institution toward them and can carry all the way through to the project level. Project stakeholders may not respect intellectual property rights, may fail to protect information, and may operate under the radar as a way to get back at their employer.

6. *Reliance on technology*: It is no surprise that information technology plays an important role in businesses today, at both the strategic and operational levels. With its rise have come greater demands for data and information to plan, execute, and monitor performance. Not only does this bring great rewards if employed effectively and efficiently, but it also leads to ethical situations and transgressions. Project stakeholders can use the technology to spy on individuals and organizations alike, to steal critical information, to discredit individuals and organizations, or to sabotage an organization's infrastructure by introducing viruses.

4.2 ADAPTING TO GLOBAL TRENDS

These trends are increasingly putting pressure on project managers to deal with ethical challenges to an unprecedented degree. If they do not respond to them or do so in a way that increases the challenges, they will find themselves unable to manage their projects effectively. Here are nine major actions to consider when dealing with the challenges that the trends pose:

1. *Determine whether the challenge affects a strategic priority*: Some project decisions and actions are more important than others. If project managers do not weigh the priority vis-à-vis ethical importance, they will be constantly dealing with ethical dilemmas and never manage their project. A priority that is strategic in nature might be a decision or action that affects the achievement of a major goal or objective of a project. Some ethical dilemmas may transcend strategic priority, such as racial discrimination or embezzlement.

But short of these, project managers need to determine if a strategic priority outweighs the importance of an ethical dilemma.

2. *Review due diligence*: Project managers determine the necessary disciplines, e.g., policies, procedures, processes, tools, and techniques related to ethics that should be in place for their project to deal with an ethical situation or transgression. They and the other stakeholders should also determine if sufficient breadth and depth exist to have prevented an ethical situation and transgression and, if so, whether they were adequate enough.

3. *Review due care*: A project can have all the disciplines in place and still not apply them during a project's execution. Occasionally, an ethical situation or transgression exists because of deliberate or benign neglect of disciplines. In other words, little or no effort is made to apply them in the project environment. It is similar to building a schedule and then not following it; it is merely window dressing. The same circumstance can apply to ethical disciplines; they merely exist as a lip service or to placate the auditors. The key is for project managers to link due diligence and due care in their review of an ethical situation or transgression to ensure follow-through.

4. *Look for compliance*: The focus of compliance is very narrow and legally oriented. Project managers and other key stakeholders should review ethical dilemmas to see whether certain laws apply and, if they do, whether all pertinent laws are being complied with. Not every ethical dilemma involves violating laws; that determination needs to be made. If a law has been violated, the right stakeholders need to be involved to ensure that corrective action occurs to mitigate or avoid fines, penalties, and perhaps even imprisonment.

5. *Take a trustee perspective*: Project managers need to take the perspective that they are trustees, or agents, for their company. While they may not be a formal manager in the organization, their organization has put resources under their care to deliver a project or service in a way that upholds that trust. This involves ensuring not only that the resources are applied efficiently and effectively but also in a manner that is done ethically. Project managers can commit an act that breaches trust, e.g., not reporting project status honestly.

6. *Confront ethical dilemmas*: When an ethical dilemma arises, it is best to confront it. That is, the project manager should take it head on and not hope that it will go away or that no one will say anything. The reality is that often, like all problems, ethical dilemmas not dealt

with early on will only continue to worsen and erupt at the wrong time. Failure to act endangers not only the organization but also the people involved. Project managers need to determine up front the who, what, when, where, why, and how of an ethical dilemma to prevent it from getting out of control.

7. *Maintain credibility*: When dealing with an ethical dilemma, project managers need to take the high road. They cannot appear biased or pursuing hidden motives. They need to act in an honest, straightforward manner. If at any time project managers appear to lose their objectivity, independence, and integrity when dealing with an ethical dilemma, stakeholders will start to question their motives. If that should occur, and it can happen quite easily and unknowingly, then they will need to seek outside help to deal with the situation.

8. *Implement corrective action*: Project managers will need to take corrective action to resolve an ethical dilemma; simply being aware is not enough. They need to get with the affected stakeholders—if no legal requirements preclude them from doing so—and come up with a plan to address the ethical dilemma. An appropriate approach is to apply the Plan-Do-Check-Act cycle (Figure 4.1), which provides a structure for dealing with and resolving ethical concerns. Of course, if the ethical dilemma is being handled by outside parties, then project managers can do nothing but observe.

9. *Ensure congruence between beliefs and behavior*: Project managers need to ensure that they walk the talk, meaning that their beliefs about ethics are manifested through their behavior. They cannot hold people to standards that they do not follow themselves. It is poor project management and poor leadership. If people see

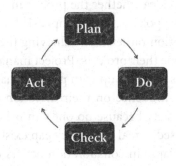

FIGURE 4.1
PDCA cycle.

hypocrisy, they will not follow project managers' guidance and will likely not participate willingly in resolving ethical situations and transgressions.

4.3 STRAYING FROM THE HIGH ROAD

Project managers constantly face pressures and challenges that test their ethical resiliency, often with limited or no authority, and yet are expected to deliver results that satisfy some powerful stakeholders. Fortunately, most project managers take the high road by dealing with ethical dilemmas in the appropriate way; the key question is why do some take an inappropriate route?

4.3.1 Organizational Perversities or Dysfunctions

The working environment is replete with confusion, wasted effort, and fear. One cause is typically poor allocation of resources, making it difficult to plan and causing a focus on outmaneuvering competition for those resources rather than achieving goals and objectives. A second cause is the misalignment of projects with the strategies of the organization at large, resulting in a project supporting priorities that lack justification and that could receive the axe at any time. The third cause is incompetence among senior leadership, which involves shifting organizational changes, the inability to focus, and little or no oversight over performance.

As you might suspect, this environment is ripe for ethical dilemmas facing project managers. To survive, project managers, not knowing whom to trust and having no idea whether the project matters to the right people, encourage negative politics. Their emphasis becomes one of seeking acceptance or justification rather than achieving the goals and objectives of their project, let alone their projects. Project managers, team members, and other stakeholders may end up with projects that lack efficacy, meaning that they have no influence on their direction or execution. Added to this is a lack of veracity because no one can believe in anything anyone has said or promised; a real credibility gap exists and starts to widen as each day passes. A lapse in collaboration occurs inside and outside of the project because no one can count on anyone being held accountable or responsible.

Naturally, project managers and other stakeholders feel that they may need to override ethical considerations to survive. Some examples include project managers exaggerating requests for resources, massaging reports in such as a way that masks the truth, falsifying reports to survive budget cuts or to outmaneuver other projects, and not making a decision for fear of getting in trouble.

There are several options for dealing with this challenge:

- Generate reports that contain reliable facts and data, meaning that the contents are verified several times for reliability and validity.
- Have key stakeholders review reports and approve them.
- Confront issues early on despite their unpopularity.

4.3.2 Tone at the Top

Members of senior leadership set the tone that permeates the entire fabric of an organization. When the tone is negative or uncaring, the rest of the organization, down to the project level, will likely be affected. The focus here is uncaring.

An uncaring management manifests itself in several ways. First, it is nonengaged in the daily operations of the organization, and this attitude carries all the way down to the project and even subproject levels. Second, accountability and responsibility are practically nonexistent; no one assumes ownership of results and sometimes even when the results are positive because, ultimately, no one cares. Third, key decisions are delayed or never made; senior managers have "higher priorities" over what is happening below their levels. Finally, changing leadership occurs, resulting in a lack of stability that, in turn, causes lack of prioritizing and direction.

This environment paves the way for ethical dilemmas to arise. People in general lose interest in what they are doing. Their focus becomes more on protecting and advancing themselves than on achieving the goals and objectives on their project. Some people may find it as an opportunity to pursue interests at the expense of the project, such as a second job. Other people may feel that whatever they do does not matter and thereby exhibit a lack of interest in the project.

Projects managers can find dealing with ethical dilemmas under these circumstances difficult when members of management are negative and micromanaging the project. Project managers may carelessly prepare reports that contain incorrect or skewed information. They may not bother to implement effective project governance disciplines because none of it appears to have any value. They can also be nonchalant toward team members who stretch the limits of ethical boundaries while on the job.

There are several options for dealing with this challenge:

- Keep key stakeholders engaged by sending reports and other documents on a regular basis to encourage and maintain involvement.
- Invite key stakeholders to attend key meetings, including ones at the project level.
- Implement good governance procedures, tools, and techniques for the project which require the involvement of key stakeholders.
- Meet regularly with key stakeholders to keep them informed and to obtain feedback on how to improve or maintain project performance.

4.3.3 Pressure to Report Only Positive Data

The pressure to report only positive information is immense, especially when money is involved. It can happen so that companies can raise stock prices or, in the project environment, when stakes are high on a project's outcome.

This pressure can be caused by many things. First, people are often rewarded for providing "good" information and not rewarded for providing "bad" information, which may reveal a less than desirable result and may provide an opportunity for someone to deny the messenger a bonus. Second, the organizational hierarchy may be so traditional or unyielding that to report anything other than positive is career suicide. Finally, the pressure to achieve certain results, such as a metric, may be so strong that people feel compelled to distort a message or cover up results to avoid retribution by those with a vested interest in achieving a specific result.

This environment creates the potential for ethical situations and transgressions in several ways. It causes people to cover up mistakes in an effort to look good. It fosters an atmosphere of fear in which numbers are massaged to avoid punishment. It encourages people to blame other people for negative or less than expected results.

Project managers can find themselves in an ethical bind. To avoid dealing with the truth, they begin to play games with the facts and data. They may, for instance, do watermelon reporting, which involves giving the impression that everything is going according to plans, but if someone digs deeper that is not really the case. Project managers may not use tools or techniques for fear their use may reveal less than desirable performance. For example, a project manager may elect to manage with a milestone schedule at a very high level to cover up significant slides rather than use techniques like earned value.

There are several options for dealing with this challenge:

- Ensure that whatever data and information are available for reports are reliable and valid, meaning scrubbing and cleansing the data prior to inclusion.
- Be consistent and persistent in reporting, meaning that the reports do not make exceptions to content and that they are developed and distributed on a regular basis.
- Have key stakeholders, such as the customer and the sponsor, review the reports prior to their release, not only to verify the data and information but also to generate support for the reports, good or bad.

4.3.4 Faster Results

Getting products to market faster than the competitor can make the difference between being the leading company in a market and being the second or even just a participant. Speed seems to be the addiction for just about everything. The project environment is no different; achieving results faster seems to be the norm. For example, several years ago a 3-year project was considered quite normal in the information technology environment. Today, few projects are allowed to last longer than 6 months and rarely more than 18 months.

There are several causes for this circumstance, one already mentioned: pressure to beat competition in the market place. A second cause is the pressure on senior management to achieve results quickly. When projects are the centerpiece for achieving those results, the pressure can be immense. Sarbanes-Oxley is a perfect example, where firms rushed to achieve satisfactory results in a relatively short period of time; otherwise, the stock value of a company could plummet and the careers of certain executives could face a similar fate.

This environment could lead to ethical dilemmas. The pressure to speed can cause burnout, putting undue pressure on certain individuals as opposed to others. If the Pareto rule applies, 80 percent sit around as they watch the other 20 percent operate at an unrelenting pace to meet an aggressive deadline, often sharing in the same rewards as those who worked the fastest and hardest. Other individuals make mistakes and do not bother to fix them, knowing that an unrealistic schedule takes precedence over quality; someone else may have to deal with the problems, for example, sometimes customers who received a product that they thought met their needs.

Project managers can find themselves taking a different route than the high road to deliver faster results. To deliver results faster, they may find they have no other choice but to circumvent standards or requirements to deliver a flawed product or service to meet a date, hoping either that no one discovers it or that they can pass it off later in the product life cycle. Taking advantage of the Pareto rule, they may put pressure on a select group of individuals and then forget about their contribution to the project and claim all the credit.

There are several options for dealing with this challenge:

- Institute project management disciplines, tools, and techniques in a manner that is scaled to the needs of the project, and insist that the team follows them.
- Include quality in the processes for building the final deliverable rather than have people pump output that results only in rework.
- Develop alternatives and a recommendation based on options analysis to determine the most efficient and effective way to complete a project.

4.3.5 No Trade-Offs between Efficiency and Effectiveness

Members of management see no relationship between cost and schedule. Both are considered important. This places extreme pressure on the project manager and the team.

There are several causes to this scenario. First, senior management faces both cost and schedule pressures, which in turn permeate all other activities. The second cause is that senior managers may be unrealistic in their demands; in other words, they are in denial by not realizing that the business world is often a series of trade-offs among assets; rarely are cost, schedule, and quality balanced. One often yields to the achievement of one or two of the others. The third cause is that senior managers commit unrealistically to a set of goals and objectives to placate higher management or the shareholders and then pressure the remainder of the organization to make it happen without the corresponding level of support.

The environment naturally lends itself to ethical situations and transgressions. The pressure is immense to deliver and encourages stakeholders to cut corners to save time and money. Everyone scrambles about almost erratically to accomplish something without concern for anything else but cost and schedule.

Project managers can find themselves in a difficult ethical situation. They may succumb to pressure to accept an unrealistic plan, both in terms of cost and schedule. They may find themselves knowingly allowing poor quality of work to exist in the hope of meeting unrealistic targets. They may not bother to put project management techniques and disciplines into place; if they do, they may not have the breadth and depth to do the job.

There are several options for dealing with this challenge:

- Come back with an options analysis and recommendation on a realistic approach toward a project; by doing so, stakeholders will then know what the risks are and share in the responsibility if the project fails.
- Generate and distribute reports on a consistent basis to provide visibility of the cost and schedule slides so that key stakeholders see the impacts of their unrealistic demands.

4.3.6 Transglobal Operations

In today's environment, businesses work on an international scale inconceivable just 50 years ago. This growth in international business has led to a wave of global projects that go beyond, for instance, the oil and gas industry. IT, manufacturing, and pharmaceutical projects are other examples where projects cross international boundaries.

There are several causes for this circumstance to arise. One is the growth of international capital, originating not just from the United States but also in other financial centers of the world. Another reason is the rise of communications and transportation to transcend time and distance. Still another reason is the decline of communism and the embrace of the capitalist ideology. The causes are countless.

These transglobal operations provide, without much effort, opportunities for ethical dilemmas on a project. Stakeholders may find themselves lacking the diverse background of working with other cultures, thereby embracing ethnocentrism, which can result in mistreating and disrespecting the beliefs and values of others. It can lead to engaging in business practices that may not be acceptable to the home office. It can lead to ignoring customs of other cultures, such as holy days for certain religions, thereby aggravating relationships.

Project managers can end up in difficult ethical circumstances in a transglobal environment. To meet cost and schedule targets, they may engage in business practices that may violate their country's laws and regulations. They may disrespect other people's cultural beliefs and values to meet those same targets. They may have to take actions that are less than ethical, but not illegal, to accommodate costs impacted by factors not in their control (e.g., currency fluctuations). They may be asked to act in a way that violates local customs and laws. They may also perform corporate espionage on partners for a transglobal project.

There are several options for dealing with this challenge:

- Become more sensitive to different cultures, such as by attending diversity training and having others do the same.
- Factor in cultural differences in their plans, such as accounting for different perceptions of time.
- Become more sensitive to home and other country legal requirements related to projects.

4.3.7 Diffusion of Accountability and Authority

Despite the rise of large organizations, particularly in the marketplace, many of them operate in a decentralized manner, making it difficult to describe accountability and authority in a sufficient manner. As a result, coordination, collaboration, and communication can be difficult, especially at the project level.

Several causes are attributed to this circumstance. First, the largeness of institutions makes it difficult to manage operations and activities down to the lowest level; sheer size necessitates delegation and decentralization. Second, the rise of large international corporations requires that they be flexible in how they conduct business, and a decentralized structure enables that to happen. They can adapt to changing conditions, too, for example, by buying and purchasing other entities.

This diffusion of accountability and authority, of course, is a double-edged sword. It provides an environment whereby some people feel that they can act, for example, as an agent on behalf of the organization when they do not have that right to do so. Without adequate oversight, they can involve themselves in less than ethical activities with the hope of never being discovered.

Project managers can find themselves in ethical dilemmas, too, but often as victims. It may be difficult to track the performance of others on their project, especially if they work on the other side of the planet. It also may be close to impossible to track a single contact point to resolve an issue because the team is so globally widespread. The same can be said for finding the right stakeholders to make key decisions. Above all, they may find it difficult to hold anyone on the team responsible to achieve specific results because the functions or processes to complete even a simple deliverable are dispersed.

There are several options for dealing with this challenge:

- Define roles, responsibilities, and authorities up front, and build definitive responsibility assignment matrices.
- Create an organizational structure that is reflected in an organization chart.
- Assign one person responsible for reporting progress for activities involving multiple resources.
- Ensure that visibility of responsibilities occurs and continues by reviewing them at the start of project meetings.

4.3.8 Obedience to Authority

This may be a contradiction to the previous challenge, but it remains an issue. In traditional organizations, especially stovepipe ones adhering to Theory X, perception about people and authority of executives and senior managers can be so strong that the project manager is simply a figurehead for a project. Instead, most of the decision making and execution of the project are done by the sponsor or members of a steering team.

There are several causes for this obedience to authority. First, people may prefer it because it acts as a convenient way to upwardly delegate responsibility, especially if something goes wrong. Second, individuals who have power very rarely want to relinquish it. In addition, senior management and executives do not trust the rank-and-file employees, who include project managers. They will likely construe taking charge as micromanaging.

The consequences of this are many. First, as mentioned already, people will upwardly delegate by shrugging off any sense of responsibility.

Second, some people will prefer to operate under the radar for fear of retribution should they think outside the box or take a chance. Third, it causes people to hoard information rather than share it. Fourth, few people are willing to take responsibility for their actions and instead blame others to protect themselves.

Project managers can find themselves in an ethical bind. They may be reluctant to raise ethical concerns for fear that they, too, will be held responsible for any transgression. They may be reluctant to make any decisions until they receive direction from senior management. They may find themselves constantly painting a rosy picture when the facts and data tell a different story. Or they may rarely take responsibility for negative results but instead may blame other people or organizations for circumstances.

There are several options for dealing with this challenge:

- Generate reports that contain irrefutable evidence about the status of a project.
- Perform a risk analysis of any commanded decisions, and communicate that risk to the appropriate stakeholders, thereby having them share in the responsibility of the results.
- Bring in other experts who may provide a different insight to the project, countering the impact of powerful stakeholders.

4.3.9 Overemphasis on Legal Compliance

Compliance is just one slice of the continuum called ethics, albeit an important one. It is important because of the ramifications for violating laws and regulations. Failure to comply can mean fines, misdemeanor or felony charges, jail sentences, disbarment, even damage to reputation. However, when compliance gets the brunt of the attention at the expense of other ethical concerns, then the nonlegal concerns can surface and cause just as much harm to an organization or project.

Fines and penalties are just one cause for overemphasis on compliance. Just as important, especially for government contractors, is disbarment from future contracts with governmental organizations. In other words, it can involve a loss of future revenue. There is another cause, too. This type of ethical dilemma is more tangible than most others. It is easier to detect than others, like harassment or soiling a person's reputation or deliberate lack of productivity to sabotage a project. In soft ethics cases, often the victim leaves or removes himself from the circumstance.

The consequences of this circumstance are that people will focus on the more immediate, tangible ethical situations or transgressions because they will be impacted in some measurable way. Another consequence is that some participants on the project will focus more on covering themselves than getting the work done for fear of being fined or going to prison. One additional consequence is that people will simply go through the motions of compliance without really appreciating the value of the law or regulation. In other words, the goal is to get the government off their backs.

Project managers can find themselves crossing the boundaries of ethical behavior in several ways. They may intentionally overlook soft ethical concerns and concentrate solely on the ones with legal ramifications. They know that a fine or prison sentence often speaks louder than a slap on the hand for allowing a minor ethical transgression. They may simply go through the motions to satisfy the government and make management happy, yet they truly do not invest much time and effort to inculcate behaviors and values that will prevent violation of the law. Ethics training in many large companies is treated as simply the "flavor of the month" program. Not surprising, even after receiving training, an ethical violation occurs, attesting to the ineffectiveness of the training.

There are several options for dealing with this challenge:

- Look at the larger picture of an ethical situation or transgression—that is, at areas that go beyond the legal arena.
- Raise these larger issues at project meetings not only to identify impacts but also to encourage people's sensitivity of ethical situations and transgressions from a much broader perspective.
- Bring in outside experts who will not only look at the legal considerations but also at others (e.g., cost and schedule performance, customer relationships).

4.3.10 Conflicting Laws and Regulations

Companies within and outside of the United States face this challenge. Within the United States, the laws often conflict from state to state. Outside the United States, the laws among countries also conflict. What is permissible in the way of doing business in one country, for example, may not be the same in another. In recent years, this challenge has intensified, making ethical decision making difficult.

There are several causes for this challenge. First, a greater fragmentation of the international community has occurred with the collapse of the Soviet Union. Second, more countries are instituting greater governmental involvement in economic affairs. Third, the laws and regulations of these countries often change when new political leadership comes into power.

The consequences of this circumstance are that individuals find it difficult to maintain a contemporary knowledge of all the laws and regulations. They also find that they are in frequent violation of some law in one country while compliant in another. They can also find themselves so busy trying to comply with the law that they lose time that could have been spent performing the real work of the project.

Project managers can end up in ethical dilemmas without ever realizing it. They may find that they have to comply with laws that seem unreasonable from a project perspective, meaning that the legalities actually jeopardize cost and schedule performance. Facing such pressures, they may circumvent the laws under extreme pressure from their senior management. They also may discover that procurement efforts are impeded by laws and thus may take shortcuts in the process that could eventually get them in trouble.

There are several options for dealing with this challenge:

- Contact the legal or ethics departments whenever a question arises about interpreting or clarifying a law.
- Access historical data and lessons learned from previous projects on how similar issues were handled in the past.
- Avoid becoming a "latrine lawyer" by acting like an expert on the law; when in doubt, check with the legal department.
- Become knowledgeable about the organization's policies and procedures in regards to dealing with other governments and laws; in fact, the entire team should become knowledgeable, too.

4.3.11 Conflict of Interest and Conflicting Interest

Increasingly, the issue of conflict of interest and conflicting interest has received more visibility in recent years. Conflict of interest occurs when individuals in a position within an organization must make or carry out decisions while potentially or actually impairing their independence and objectivity. Conflicting interest occur when personal activities interfere with their responsibilities on another job, resulting in diluting their degree of dedication and commitment.

Conflict of interest is of concern nowadays because legal requirements play an increasingly important role due to greater shareholder involvement in governance, such as required under Sarbanes-Oxley. Second, the relationship of government and business has gotten more intertwined over the last several decades, drawing more attention to areas like procurement management where even the mere appearance of a conflict of interest can be problematic.

Awareness of conflicting interest has risen as well, mainly because in the current economic climate workforce job security has declined; thus, more and more people are getting side jobs to sustain their lifestyles in case they lose their main job. Sometimes, these side jobs can become so lucrative that employees cannot fulfill their responsibilities.

In this environment, project managers can face ethical dilemmas. From a conflict of interest perspective, they may find that their previous experience with an employer or investments may set the stage for them to lose their objectivity and independence when making decisions or carrying out the plans of the project. They may inadvertently make a decision that violates a law or company policy. From a conflicting interest perspective, they may have side consulting businesses that could draw their attention away from fulfilling their responsibilities as a project manager.

There are several options for dealing with this challenge:

- Become more knowledgeable about the pertinent laws, regulations, policies, and procedures related to conflicts of interest and conflicting interests, especially when it comes to government contracts.
- Encourage the participation of the procurement organization on projects to oversee compliance with the laws, regulations, policies, and procedures related to conflicts of interest.
- Have ethics on the agenda for ongoing team meetings.

4.3.12 Pressure to Adjust Results to Meet Expectations

Sometimes, perhaps oftentimes, executives and senior management make commitments that set expectations so high that it puts tremendous pressure on the people doing the work to meet them. These expectations can be so unrealistic that when reality hits home people are fearful of reporting the truth. This is a prescription for failure for project managers, who are afterward found in an indefensible position.

There are many causes for this circumstance. One is top-down management style, which fails to ask people first what is required to get the job done. Second, key stakeholders may have rose-colored glasses that filter any data and information that refute their decisions. Third, incentive programs for executive and managers can put tremendous pressure on them to achieve near impossible results, which in turn puts pressure on the project manager to do the same. Finally, senior and executive management may be involved in groupthink, which puts considerable pressure on people to distort reality.

When faced with this challenge, people act in ways that cannot help but lead to disaster. They begin to cut corners. They are so fearful of failure that they play it safe by doing only what they have been directed to do. They may not be truthful about their progress.

Project managers can find themselves in an ethical situation. They may experience pressure to report only positive results or to manipulate data. They may try to shift responsibility for not meeting expectations by pointing fingers at team members.

There are several options for dealing with this challenge:

- Design and deploy a project information repository that is populated with reliable data, meaning that its contents enable the generation of useful reports on the status of their projects. Good data become irrefutable, no matter the pressure. As Alan Mullaly, head of Ford, said, "The data will set you free."
- Generate a consistent set of reports that people can use to track performance over time, making it difficult for one or a few stakeholders to sway their contents.
- Make results visible as often as possible, such as through a project web site or a portal.
- Go to the legal department or call a company hotline to report any pressure to have reports altered.

4.3.13 Restricted Access to Information

While at first this might not seem like an ethical dilemma, it can be one if the intent is to mislead. Sometimes people are denied information because of the sensitivity or controversial nature of the content.

There are several reasons for this challenge. First, management may restrict access to information because if people know in advance that the budget for the project is going to be reduced, perhaps because it no longer supports the strategic goals and objectives of the higher organization, they may no longer concentrate on their work and may focus on finding another job. Second, executive and senior management may want to protect intellectual property or proprietary information, especially if the project could lead to a significant competitive advantage.

There are consequences, of course, to restricting access to information. Stakeholders, especially the ones doing the work, may feel resentful about not being trusted to have information. Some stakeholders may not be able to communicate or collaborate effectively.

Project managers may find themselves in an ethical bind. They may know information that could negatively affect the financial well-being of team members yet may not be at liberty to share critical information about what could impact them. They could generate reports that tell only part of a story, potentially misleading people as to the project's and consequently team members' fate. Under such circumstances, the project manager is placed in an unenviable position of having a responsibility to the team and maintaining the trust and confidence of senior or executive management.

There are several options for dealing with this challenge:

- Take inventory of data and information and determine which need to be protected and which do not; content of the latter will require controlled access.
- Determine controlled access, which will help to preclude the release of intellectual property and other proprietary information to the wrong individuals or organizations.
- Take actions to ensure open dialogue and sharing of information on the project during meetings, and post information on a web site or some other medium. The key is to determine what can be shared and what requires restrictive access.

4.3.14 Reduced Cycle Time

Reinventing the wheel, whether in the office or a manufacturing facility, is a waste of time and energy. It is best if a project can capitalize on the work of previous projects to accomplish expeditious goals and objectives.

However, sometimes pressure to reduce cycle time comes from upper management, which can lead to ethical dilemmas.

There are many reasons for this challenge. First, tremendous cost pressures may lead people to falsely believe that faster equals cheaper. Second, it is considered good practice to not reinvent the wheel because doing so only lengthens the cycle time to complete work. Third, the desire to deliver a product or service ahead of the competition can inadvertently or unintentionally introduce errors or defects.

When cycle time is reduced, sometimes corners are cut to deliver a product or service, thus circumventing quality standards. For example, team members may deliberately release a product offering features or functions the customer wants, but doing so may result in considerable problems rework later, such as during sustaining and maintenance.

Project managers can find themselves in an ethical complication. They may allow the team to circumvent standards of quality to satisfy the need to reduce cycle time. They may reuse material to which another company owns the patent rights or copyrights to cut down on cycle time.

There are several options for dealing with this challenge:

- Document project processes, such as management plans, and ensure that people use and follow them during projects.
- Streamline processes.
- Build quality in processes to ensure that there is less emphasis on inspection.
- Institute controls (e.g., thresholds, metrics) to trigger when reviews are necessary.
- Implement cross-checking of people's work, keeping in mind that this may add to the cycle time. Therefore, these cross-checks should occur only for key elements of the product or service being delivered.

4.3.15 Increased Customer Satisfaction

Like reducing cycle time, this one seems innocent. Yet, like reducing cycle time, it can lead to ethical dilemmas in an effort to please the customer.

There are several causes for this challenge. First, because of international competition, first from Japan and now from China and India, the competition for customer satisfaction now plays an instrumental role in winning and sustaining business. Second, business retention in a changing world actually stabilizes revenue generation and allows for concentrating on expanding market presence. Third, customer satisfaction is good public relations.

Sometimes, increasing customer satisfaction encourages people to act in a way that might be construed as an ethical situation or transgression. Team members may cave in to an unrealistic or faulty request that could eventually lead to a defective product, thereby putting the project and customer at risk. Team members may hide potentially negative information that the customer should know about for fear of alienating the customer.

Project managers may be under even more pressure to satisfy the customer. They may find that their management uses metrics to gauge customer satisfaction; good results in metrics may bring positive rewards, thereby encouraging positive reporting rather than negative reporting. To please the customer, project managers may overlook customer requests to expand the product or service without assessing the impact to cost and schedule; however, in the long run this can escalate costs. They may also not want to confront a sensitive issue or problem for fear of upsetting the customer; instead they allow the problem to continue in the hope that it fades away but, in reality, often never does but instead gets more intense.

There are several options for dealing with this challenge:

- Implement good project management disciplines that encourage the involvement of the customer; one specific discipline is integrated change control, which, if implemented correctly, will require an impact analysis of any significant change requests.
- Engage other key stakeholders who, not being with the customer (e.g., the project sponsor), can provide a check on a customer who makes unrealistic requests.
- Provide visibility for customer requests, such as posting on a web site, so that other stakeholders can review them and make recommendations.

4.3.16 Stress on Becoming a Team Player

For projects to succeed, everyone needs to be a team player, that is, someone who can communicate and collaborate with one another to achieve a common vision. Without team players, a project is nothing more than a group of people who operate independently and direct their energies and efforts toward their own goals and not necessarily those of the project. In most project environments in the corporate environment, the pressure to be a team player is immense, and to be labeled as not a team player, especially for the project manager, can prove costly from a career perspective.

There are two principal reasons for the trend toward being a team player. First, the project environment has become very specialized; any final product, such as an engineering or software project, often requires contributions from and cooperation of people from different disciplines. Second, the work environment, partly due to the downturn in the economy and the threat of outsourcing, has placed immense pressure on people to work more cooperatively and closely than ever before; the inability to work with others can lead to being identified as not a team player and, subsequently, a target for dismissal.

The pressure to be a team player can affect stakeholders' ethical behavior on a project. They may submerge their thoughts to avoid appearing too independent from the rest of the team. For example, they may disagree with the direction of the project for valid reasons but will not speak their concerns for fear of being ostracized. They may be reluctant to offer new ideas for fear of upsetting the status quo. Basically, some stakeholders will surrender their independent thoughts due to groupthink. In the end, for fear of not appearing as a team player, their communications and creativity suffer and could lead to rework.

Project managers may be susceptible to this pressure. They may feel compelled to hold back their own opinions. They may be reluctant to bring up an issue that they feel could negatively impact their relationship with the team even though they know that if they raised the issue it would improve the chances for project success. Some project managers may even suppress serious negative information to maintain at least the perception that everyone on the project team is a team player. They may even allow unethical situations and transgressions to take place so that they and others appear as team players.

There are several options for dealing with this challenge:

- Encourage team members and other stakeholders to participate in exercises such as brainstorming that require thinking outside the box.
- Bring in experts who provide a contrary perspective to current thoughts about a challenge, issue, or concern.
- Assign people to activities that encourage them to perform independently, thereby reducing the influence of peer pressure.

4.3.17 Play by the Book

Otherwise known as doing things right, this offers several advantages. It helps keep people out of trouble. It allows for people to march in the same direction. It reduces waste. Doing the right things can vary from doing things right. People comply with the rules, yet unethical behavior can still arise.

Project managers may hide behind the rules as an excuse. They may feel that the rules allow them to condone a particular behavior on their part or that of others. They may bend the rules to act in a questionable way.

Some examples include allowing some activity to occur that may be questionable from an ethical standpoint but falls within the policies and procedures of the organization; complying with the letter of the law about reporting yet suppressing key negative information because it is not required according to reporting requirements; allowing their projects to continue activities that do not add to the value of the project but that fall within the boundaries of what is permissible; and bending the rules to retaliate against individuals who disagree with the current direction of the project.

There are several options for dealing with this challenge:

- Broaden perspective on an ethical situation or transgression by looking at factors beyond compliance.
- Question the validity of the rules by encouraging people to think outside the box.
- Seek the insight of people who have no vested interest in the outcome of an ethical issue or transgression.

4.3.18 Treat Symptoms as Fact

In the contemporary project environment, the pressure to meet cost, schedule, and quality requirements can be immense. Circumstances often afford little or no time to analyze the cause of problem, no matter the topic. If project managers perform analysis, it is cursory at best. Often, the quick rather than lasting fix becomes the norm. In other words, no time is available to apply a PDCA cycle.

Naturally, treating symptoms as facts has its consequences. Short-term fixes lead to long-term problems. The project team moves into a reactive, rather than proactive, mode. Some people look at ways to reduce project costs but fail to factor in life cycle product costs. The bottom line is that it emphasizes the here and now and not the future. Ironically, a short-term fix reduces costs in the present but later increases the product life cycles. Sometimes, the fix introduces an even more complex problem during the project life cycle, impairing and possibly even altogether stopping progress.

Team members then end up in an ethical situation. They make fixes, knowing all too well that each fix will introduce a problem later that must be addressed by someone else. In other words, it encourages a lack of responsibility and accountability for results. Team members pass the buck to someone else and allow someone else to deal with the real problem. They knowingly let the customer assume costs in the postproject period that should have been assumed during the project life cycle.

Project managers can also find themselves falling into an ethical lapse. They figure that the effort will cause them more complications with the customer than if they address the problem now. They may allow a quick fix to avoid shattering the perception that the project is progressing according to expectations. They may think that a customer may not know the difference and, therefore, that it is okay to pass the issue or problems to postproject support, such as sustaining and maintenance. They may even misreport the cause of problem by downplaying its effects, knowing all too well that the consequences may be costly sometime in the future.

There are several options for dealing with this challenge*:

- Constantly ask the three-letter question why.
- Persist in applying reliable tools, such as Pareto diagrams that display data revealing what are the significant causes to a problem, to determine the real cause behind an ethical dilemma.
- Rely on facts and data, rather than on intuition or opinion, to ascertain the cause of a problem.
- Seek outside advice and opinions on dilemmas from people who do not have a vested interest in the outcome.
- Have the courage to confront ethical dilemmas regardless of the consequences because it is the right action.

---

* Rita Mulcahy, PMP Exam Prep, 6th ed. (Minnetonka, MN: RMC Publications, 2009), 285.

4.3.19 Reliance on Numbers

In some business circles, there is a prevailing belief that what cannot be measured does not matter. The emphasis is on quantified results, not on feelings, intuition, hearsay, or assumptions. The numbers become the focus and, though they are objective, they can lead to ethical dilemmas.

There are many reasons for the emphasis on numbers. First, there is at least the perception that numbers are tangible and, hence, objective, although the assumptions driving the numbers must be examined to ensure that some degree of objectivity is maintained. Second, numbers are tangible, and intuition, feelings, and hearsay are not—they tend to be highly subjective and mushy. Third, the quality movement in the last 3 decades has emphasized metrics and measures and the use of tools to generate them. Finally, as mentioned earlier, people think that unmeasured work is inconsequential, because measurement provides focus and feedback.

The emphasis on numbers can place people in ethical dilemmas. Numbers could end up justifying behavior or actions that under ordinary circumstances would be considered unethical. Numbers can be the primary focus on reaching certain metrics but not necessarily provide a quality product—in other words, cause people to have some degree of myopia.

Some project managers emphasize numbers at the expense of ethics. Their focus could be on achieving numerical results rather than on the vision, goals, and objectives of their projects. They could actually alter their reports to give a skewed view of the state of their projects. Project managers may intentionally or inadvertently overlook nonmeasurable concerns that could be just as important as numeric considerations, thereby skewing reporting.

There are several options for dealing with this challenge:

- Make a special effort to look beyond the numbers by considering softer areas that can relate to ethical concerns, such as attitudes, beliefs, and assumptions.
- Talk to people inside and outside the projects to see if insights corroborate the numbers.
- Review the numbers themselves to question their validity and reliability; sometimes the data are flawed and are used to generate information; flawed data equal flawed information, which in turn can lead to flawed decisions.

4.3.20 Desire for Agreement

The larger the project, generally the more difficult it is to achieve agreement for the simple reason that larger audiences have a greater diversity of mind and body. While agreement is good, it is very difficult to attain; agreement means that everyone must accept everything as is. Unfortunately, agreement is often confused with consensus, which essentially means that a person may not consent to something completely but understands the general idea and agrees to support it.

The desire for agreement has several origins. The concept of teamwork, so important in project management, often gets confused with having complete agreement. Consequently, nothing moves forward on a project because not everyone agrees. Another contributor is the contemporary emphasis on horizontal communications; often people confuse agreement with feedback, thinking because someone disagrees or has questions with some data or information in a message nothing can move forward until the discrepancy is resolved. The desire for collaboration can be a cause, too, because it requires people communicating with each other regularly; if agreement is not reached, then progress may come to a halt. Finally, the desire for unity of direction necessitates at least some degree of agreement; failure to achieve agreement, as opposed to consensus, can cause a project to come to a halt.

The desire for consensus on a project can cause people in general to stretch ethical limits. They inhibit expressing themselves when they should be doing otherwise for the good of the project. They may share data or information but in a way that either discounts or clouds the real message. They could also avoid taking the initiative for fear of upsetting team members or other stakeholders.

Project managers could present data or information in a way that may not communicate the severity of a situation. They may not take the initiative to resolve issues if they find that certain stakeholders may disagree. They may feel inhibited in expressing their thoughts or ideas for fear of any disagreement arising, such as at a key point in the project life cycle. Worse, they may be coming up for an evaluation that requires the input of stakeholders and may not want to bring up controversial issues or other topics that could tarnish it.

There are several options for dealing with this challenge:

- Play the devil's advocate whenever an issue or concern related to an ethical situation or transgressions is discussed.
- By acting as an advocate for a position, hopefully encourage open, insightful discussion that shatters people's assumptions or paradigms.

- Bring in outside experts to provide insights and raise issues that internal stakeholders, including the project manager, might not want to raise and address.
- Seek consensus instead of agreement; consensus means understanding, acceptance, and support despite not agreeing totally; seeking consensus will help avoid stalemate over an issue or concern.
- Encourage initiative and independent thinking by setting an atmosphere in projects that tolerates dissent and different viewpoints.
- Meet one on one with people to get new insights that would not ordinarily be obtained in a group meeting.

4.3.21 Maintain Positive Working Relationships with Vendors, Partners, and Other External Stakeholders

As mentioned earlier, the pressure to be a team player can be immense. It is critical to the success of a project. It is critical to success as a project manager. It can be critical with other stakeholders, such as vendors and partners. This relationship is especially important when the project must deliver a product to the customer. Most projects, especially medium-sized and large ones, depend on an array of relationships internal and external to achieve their vision, goals, and objectives. When any or all of these relationships go awry, they can seriously impact the progress of a project.

There are several contributors to the pressure to maintain a working relationship with vendors, partners, and other external stakeholders. The globalization of businesses in general and projects in particular is one contributor. Another one is the rise of outsourcing to produce significant deliverables. Finally, the rise of manufacturing concepts such as just-in-time, supply chain, and Lean encourage greater working relationships to ensure products and services arrive when needed at the right time and in the right quantity.

Oddly enough, the desire to maintain working relationships with vendors, partners, and other stakeholders can lead to ethical complications for some people. Some people may intentionally or inadvertently become too cozy in their relationships to the point that it affects their objectivity. Some people may see vendors or partners as an eventual opportunity to increase their pay down the road, thereby clouding their judgment.

Some project managers are vulnerable to the same ethical complications. In addition to ending up in cozy relationships with vendors and partners, they also may skew reports without even realizing it. They may be impacted by what is known as the halo effect, whereby one characteristic overshadows all the others; wining and dining on a regular basis at the expense of vendors or partners is one way to make that happen.

There are several options for dealing with this challenge:

- Insist that vendors and partners report regularly using facts and data; opinion and intuition are not enough on either side. Facts and data in reports keep the relationships from deteriorating into an accusatorial relationship.
- Build a team, not adversarial, relationship. It is all too easy for a large company with plenty of money to get arrogant with its partners and vendors. When arrogance takes hold then accusations of, for example, poor performance or dishonesty arise on both sides, resulting in lack of cooperation and collaboration. Building a team relationship includes having suppliers and vendors in meetings for planning and managing projects
- Set up a joint infrastructure that enables open dialogue for sharing information and resolving differences.
- Make the relationship with them visible. You can ensure that successes and failures are shared alike.

4.3.22 Protecting One's Status and Position

Survival is a strong instinct, and when it comes to the protection of one's livelihood it can of course cause people to take to act in ways that stretch or break ethical limits.

In recessionary periods, the threats to livelihoods are commonplace. Raising an ethical issue can mean doing the right thing but can also lead to job loss. The fate of whistle-blowers in the news is often described as falling on a grenade; however noble the action, the results can be devastating. Of course, another force causes people to stretch or break ethical limits: outsourcing. In a world of globalization, many varieties of outsourcing arrangement are made that may and frequently do result in people losing their livelihoods. Consequently, people are put in ethical situations or transgressions: save oneself or allow an ethical situation or transgression to arise or continue?

Team members can react to this challenge in certain ways. They can turn their heads, so to speak, to unethical dilemmas, simply by pretending they do not exist. They can become a participant in the unethical decision or action, thinking that the benefits of participating outweigh the costs of being caught. They can, of course, become a whistle-blower.

Project managers also can end up in ethical complications. They, too, can pretend that the ethical dilemma does not exist. They can become a willing participant, weighing the costs and benefits. They can manipulate the data and information in reports to hide the ethical dilemma. They can encourage peer pressure to lessen the opportunity of an individual becoming a whistle-blower or taking the initiative to deal with the challenge.

There are several options for dealing with this challenge:

- Establish and maintain open, ongoing communications, which means revealing negative information, with stakeholders; this approach is the surest way to demonstrate dedication to projects and not just to career.
- Keep an audit trail of decisions and actions about projects; this option allows for protecting everyone involved.
- Establish and maintain open communications to serve as a check to anyone threatening someone else about their careers.

4.4 FINAL THOUGHTS

Project managers and their projects increasingly no longer operate in isolation. Trends across the globe are impacting local projects in planning and executing in ways never before imagined. As the scope of a project increases in terms of size and complexity, the greater the likelihood that these global trends will need to be considered because they can have ethical implications. Project managers will then have to be proactive rather than reactive in ethical situations as they try to deal with these global concerns.

4.5 GETTING STARTED CHECKLIST

Question		Yes	No
1.	Have you considered how the following large-scale trends could potentially cause unethical issues to arise on your project?		
	Greater globalization		
	Importance of intellectual property		
	More rights in the workplace		
	Greater regulatory oversight		
	Outsourcing		
	Reliance on technology		
2.	After considering the impact of the aforementioned global trends, have you considered, from an ethical perspective, performing the following actions?		
	Determine whether the trend affects a strategic priority		
	Review due diligence		
	Review due care		
	Look for compliance		
	Take a trustee perspective		
	Confront ethical issues and transgressions		
	Maintain your credibility		
	Implement corrective action		
	Ensure congruence between beliefs and behavior		
3.	Have you considered some of the following pressures and challenges that could lead you to stray from the high road? Have you thought about dealing with the ones that relate to you?		
	Organizational perversities		
	Tone at the top		
	Pressure to report positive data only		
	Faster results		
	No trade-offs between efficiency and effectiveness		
	Transglobal operations		
	Diffusion of accountability and authority		

Question	Yes	No
Obedience to authority		
Overemphasis on legal compliance		
Conflicting laws and regulations		
Pressure to adjust results to meet expectations		
Restrict access to information		
Reduce cycle time		
Increase customer satisfaction		
Stress on becoming a team player		
Play by the book		
Treat symptoms as fact		
Reliance on numbers		
Desire for agreement		
Maintain positive working relationships with vendors, partners, and other external stakeholders		
Protecting one's status and position		

5

How Ethics Permeates the Entire Project Life Cycle

The boardrooms across corporate America are not the only places for ethical dilemmas to arise. The context surrounding projects lays the groundwork for ethical issues to occur. The nature of the projects and their context can play a big role on how ethics is viewed by stakeholders, whether and how they incorporate it in their decision making, and whether or how they exhibit it in their behavior.

Projects have some contextual factors that provide the opportunity for forcing ethical dilemmas.

5.1 CONTEXTUAL FACTORS

1. *Temporary existence*: Projects have a short-term life and go away. Some people see them as opportunities to push ethical limits to the extreme, especially those who support projects on a contractual basis. They do what they've been tasked to do and then take off to other projects or locations, often without ever seeing the consequences of their actions. Instead, someone else will deal with the aftermath: a product manager or a customer, perhaps. Contractual workers can perform poor-quality work in a software system and someone, such as a customer, will experience the consequence in sustaining and maintenance. So why does it matter? After all, they will be gone; it's someone else's problem, they reason.

2. *Finites*: Projects exist for a specific amount of time and then stop at some point. This ending has significance in that the impending closing date can encourage people to make an expeditious fix to something and, once again, not worry about the long-term consequences. After all, they reason, they will be long gone after the project has been completed. For example, they make a quick fix to a product in the hope that nobody will know about it if a problem occurs and, if it does, the warranty costs can cover the problem.

3. *Visibility*: Projects have high visibility. At first, a project manager would think that a highly visible project would minimize any opportunity for an ethical dilemma to arise because key stakeholders and others would notice; however, a highly visible project may foster an ethical dilemma to arise. For example, the project manager could manipulate reporting data to give the perception that the project is progressing as planned when in reality it is the opposite.

4. *Time pressure*: This weight on team members can be unrelenting on a project that must deliver a product or service over a very short period, such as when the project is fast-tracked. For instance, the completion date cannot be adjusted or the company could face substantial penalty payments for late delivery. Such a circumstance can encourage members of the team to go for the quick fix or fail to meet certain specifications in the hopes that nothing will happen or if it does it would be too serious.

5. *Temporary relationships*: Project relationships among stakeholders are temporary. People come and go as required, sometimes never to return. Under such circumstances, some individuals see this as an opportunity to "stretch the limits," in the expectation that they may never get caught. For example, a project team member may knowingly be rude to another person or perform some indiscrete act knowing that they will be gone after a short while.

In all fairness, these ethical situations and transgressions are far from the norm. Although the context of a project does provide the opportunity for unethical behavior, most people do not use it as such. Many people often witness unethical behavior in the workplace. The project management environment lays the groundwork for that to happen; it does not mean ethical dilemmas will happen.

5.2 FIVE MAJOR PROJECT MANAGEMENT PROCESSES

There are five major processes of project management.

Initiating is when the vision, mission, goals, objectives, and scope of the project are defined up front in the form of a charter, statement of work, or contract or a combination of all three. Sometimes, a few of the stakeholders will engage in unethical behavior with the anticipation of gaining even more advantage once the project begins. They may not bargain in good faith, they may do some illegal competitive behavior, or they may even engage in bribery.

Planning involves determining the road map for executing the contents of the charter, statement of work, or contract or a combination of all three. It provides the opportunity for some stakeholders to engage in a few unethical practices. For example, they may not provide reliable estimates or purposely provide scheduling information that does not eventually allow tracking of performance in any meaningful way.

Executing means carrying out the plans. During this process, some stakeholders operate under the radar by not showing up at meetings, not delivering on time, or refusing to share information. Some team members may purposely underperform during working hours so they can receive overtime pay in the evening.

Monitoring and controlling means keeping abreast of how well the project is executing according to plan and in such a way that it is achieving its initial vision. Opportunities abound here for unethical situations and transgressions to arise. For example, some people may not truthfully report their hours worked on tasks, or they may purposely try to sabotage deliverables on a project for some reason (e.g., personality conflicts). Vendors may not provide timely submittals on cost and schedule status for fear of project termination or inviting an audit on their reporting.

Closing is the process of administratively and contractually concluding a project. Project managers ensure that all the terms and conditions as well as any outstanding obligations have been met. Ethical dilemmas can also arise here. The vendor may pressure the conclusion of a project to work on another more lucrative one elsewhere, thereby not completing the current work thoroughly. Or final billing statements may not be submitted for some time to avoid buyer scrutiny. Certain team members may deliberately leave the remaining tasks unattended still bill out for them as they look for another position.

These project management processes do not necessarily indicate that ethical dilemmas exist but simply provide opportunity for doing so. Project managers need to be aware that some type of unethical dilemmas could arise based on the context and processes of projects. It is also necessary to realize that not all ethical dilemmas are intentional, so people may just need to be aware of their occurrence and take any appropriate corrective actions.

5.3 CATEGORIES OF ETHICAL DILEMMAS

Because of the abstract nature of ethics, it is difficult to group ethical dilemmas into discrete categories. One effective approach, however, is to use an audit approach for categorizing management controls which usually includes five categories. These five categories of ethical topics are: (1) compliance; (2) effectiveness; (3) accurate and timely information; (4) efficiency; and (5) protection of resources.

5.3.1 Compliance

This category deals with adherence to policies, procedures, laws, and regulations. It is perhaps the most common topic of ethics about which people are knowledgeable, since penalties can be severe, can become public, and can become litigious on a personal level.

Project managers in today's environment are getting increasingly involved in compliance, thanks in part to the corporate scandals and social legislation of the last 3 decades. Greater emphasis on protection of personal information and intellectual property, environmental regulations, financial oversight, employee relations, and much more has caused project managers to look beyond just delivering a product or service to compliance and the consequences of their or other stakeholders' actions. What adds to the complexity is that some of these laws and regulations are often unclear and contradictory.

Also, the time and cost pressures can become immense, causing some people to take shortcuts to receive a bonus; however, the consequences could have far-reaching compliance issues.

5.3.2 Effectiveness

This category addresses the achievement of goals and objectives. A goal in this context is a broad statement of intent; an objective is something measurable to know when the goal has been achieved.

Effectiveness is an ethical area because project managers are responsible for achieving results with the resources entrusted to them. Using resources in a way that subverts the achievement of goals and objectives is a violation of trust. This simple relationship between goals and objectives is in reality not that simple for project managers. Goals and objectives within the project must be achieved; however, often projects are part of a much bigger organization, which requires that projects be aligned with its goals and objectives. In theory, they should be in alignment; in reality, often they are contradictory. Project managers can also find themselves in a difficult position where the higher organization's goals and objectives are at odds with the customer's.

This circumstance can place immense pressure on people and can lead to ethical dilemmas. Politics can become overwhelmingly important, so much so that some people will overcommit to some and underdeliver to others. Naturally, this can lead to circumstances where the project managers and other stakeholders find themselves providing misinformation, even disinformation, to certain stakeholders.

5.3.3 Accurate and Timely Information

This category deals with ensuring that the right people get the right information in the right amount in the right format at the right time. People often confuse information with data; the two are not synonymous. Data are raw and have no value to anyone. Information is data converted into something meaningful to the recipient. The challenge is to link data and information in a manner that ensures accurate and timely delivery of the latter.

Providing accurate and timely information is an ethical concern because many stakeholders in the project environment rely on information to make decisions. An unethical person can corrupt data that, in turn, generates unreliable information without anyone realizing it. For example, entering bogus data into a time-reporting tool that generates information for key executive stakeholders can lead to making ineffective decisions.

5.3.4 Efficiency

This category deals with using resources in a manner that reduces waste. For every unit of currency spent, ideally there should be some incremental increase in return.

Efficiency is an ethical area of concern because stakeholders have entrusted project managers with using resources in a manner that is not profligate. Projects are investments and like all investments should be managed with care. Project managers, to a certain extent, are entrusted agents for their company and are responsible for ensuring that investors in their project get the appropriate return for their money.

Opportunities abound on projects for violating the ethical side of efficiency. Some examples include individuals deliberately underperforming during regular hours to earn overtime pay in the evening. Some people take trips, affectionately referred to as *boondoggles*, that offer little or no return to the outcome of the project. Such waste demonstrates a disregard for responsibly managing the resources of projects.

5.3.5 Protection of Resources

This category is about the ethical area related to the physical and logical safekeeping of the project's resources. Physical resources deal with equipment, supplies, and other tangible assets. Logical resources pertain to nontangible items like information and intellectual property.

Protection of resources is an ethical area because, again, it involves entrusting project managers to ensure that monies invested by management and shareholders, for example, are not squandered or used inappropriately. The project environment offers opportunities for unethical transgressions. For example, some people may use information or technology for personal use during the course of the project, or they may disclose information in a manner that fails to respect the need for privacy or the protection of proprietary information, either for their own firm or for that of their partners.

5.4 ETHICS AND PROJECT MANAGEMENT PROCESSES

This section identifies some common ethical dilemmas that occur when executing each of the five process groups (i.e., initiating, planning, executing, monitoring and controlling, and closing). Each one is in turn associated with one or more of the five ethical categories. Many of these ethical dilemmas overlap; however, for purposes of the discussion, they are treated separately.

5.4.1 Initiating and Ethics

The significance of ethical dilemmas during initiating is that they can have a downstream impact on all five process groups and phases of a project and will also span across all five ethical categories (Table 5.1).

5.4.2 Low-Balling

During the initiating process of a project, stakeholders all have some interest that needs to be satisfied. In many cases, the buyer (i.e., the company

TABLE 5.1

Initiating and Ethics

	Compliance	Effectiveness	Accurate and Timely Information	Efficiency	Protection of Resources
Low-balling				√	
Omitting key stakeholders		√			
Misalignment with organizational goals		√			
Conflicts of interest	√				√
Not clarifying expectations		√		√	
Lying to win contract	√		√		
Sabotaging relationships with certain vendors		√		√	
Not engaging in good faith negotiations		√		√	

purchasing materials or services) and the seller (i.e., the company providing materials or services) seek to have an agreement. Sometimes, however, the seller may intentionally underbid with the hope of beating out competition and then, once winning the contract, will decide to change the work order to make up for the initial loss. Low-balling can, of course, have serious negative ramifications, which include a buyer feeling taken advantage of or having a sense of being misled and, perhaps most importantly, a lack of trust that permeates the entire relationship. In the end, it wastes the buyer's resources, that is, the project. If low-balling occurs at the beginning of a project it is a bad sign of what is to come.

Low-balling can be addressed by asking questions about vendor capabilities early in the negotiating process, conducting a risk assessment to determine where low-balling could occur and when it could have the biggest impact, and researching, for example, the present standards.

5.4.3 Omitting Key Stakeholders

If the intent is to purposely omit key stakeholders during the initiating phase, an ethical dilemma may be in the works. The stakeholders may be working together to bring a project into an organization through the back door; once the project is started, the other stakeholders are essentially compelled to accept, sometimes through organizational politics. The consequences include increasingly more politics in the decision making of the project, greater levels of mistrust among stakeholders, and encouragement of subtle ways to negatively impact the progress of the project. All of this can also lead to waste in terms of time, effort, and money.

Omitting key stakeholders can be addressed by conducting a thorough stakeholder analysis, creating a stakeholder register to help in performing the analysis, and working to get all the key stakeholders engaged during the initiating process by participating in the development and approval of a charter, statement of work, cost analysis, and contract formulation.

5.4.4 Misaligning with Organizational Goals

This ethical dilemma depends on intent. Sometimes an organization will start projects with the intent of achieving organizational goals and objectives. During the initiating process, a charter and other supporting documentation are developed emphasizing that the project will help accomplish the goals and objectives of the organization, when in reality it serves some other purpose. However, the organization fails eventually to provide sufficient oversight of the project. The project manager or some other stakeholder then purposely steers the project in a different direction, knowing full well the project is operating according to some other priority, perhaps the stakeholders' own goals and objectives. The consequences include a misuse of resources to achieve unintended goals and objectives.

Misalignment with organizational goals can be addressed by keeping all the stakeholders' focus on the organizational goals and objectives when developing the charter and establishing processes and procedures to verify alignment to them throughout the project life cycle.

5.4.5 Conflicting Interest

During initiating, stakeholders should not have any previous background or assets that could impair their judgment related to objectivity and independence. This is especially the case when negotiating with external stakeholders. Examples might include a stakeholder with a substantial amount of stock in a company who will be awarded a contract increasing the value of that stock. The consequences are that a conflict of interest can lead to all sorts of civil and criminal problems as well as can result in using company resources leading to personal benefit.

Conflicts of interest can be addressed by keeping people aware of the need to comply with company processes and procedures regarding that topic. These conflicts, even mere appearances of them, should be dealt with immediately to ensure that no complications arise later, such as just prior to completion of a major milestone. Of course, project managers are the main people who should avoid having a conflict of interest, because execution of their responsibilities is so tied to credibility.

5.4.6 Not Clarifying Expectations

In the beginning, all the key stakeholders have expectations. These are sometimes clearly articulated; at other times, they are vague and intentionally left so. Vague expectations can provide the opportunity for some stakeholders to exploit the working relationship vis-à-vis others. Project managers should make every effort to clarify and pinpoint expectations to ensure such exploitation does not occur. Besides helping to improve communications and allowing for focus on achieving results, clarifying expectations encourages greater levels of trust among stakeholders because the opportunity to take advantage of one of the parties lessens. The consequences of intentionally not clarifying expectations will only lead only to distrust, resulting in less focus on achieving results and waste due to always needing to verify.

Expectations can be clarified by addressed them during initiating in general and in particular when negotiating the project charter. Clarifying expectations not only enables focusing later on in the project but also provides a great way to bridge differences and maintain dialogue among all stakeholders.

5.4.7 Lying to Win Contract

Lying, misrepresentation, fabricating the truth, or whatever you call it is not a good idea during initiating. Stakeholders may get what they want in the beginning, but once lies are discovered, then the performance of the project begins to deteriorate. Distrust and mistrust, for example, will permeate the entire atmosphere surrounding the project. Not only does lying have legal consequences, but it also impacts the ability to monitor progress on a project because the data and eventual information become suspect. This results in laborious efforts to check and recheck everything regarding the status of a project once it gets implemented.

Lying to win a contract can be addressed provided that open, ongoing communications and exchange of information occurs on a project. If and when a stakeholder is being less than truthful and the project manager knows it, he has an obligation to confront the issue. Credibility is key, not just for him but among all the major stakeholders; the minute credibility is lost then suspicion takes over.

5.4.8 Sabotaging Relationships with Certain Stakeholders

In the beginning of a project, especially for those outside of a company, certain stakeholders on the project may prefer one vendor over another. During negotiations, some stakeholders may deliberately try to denigrate one vendor to give the competitive advantage to another for whatever reason (e.g., conflict of interest). The consequences are that, even if another vendor does sign an agreement, tension rises due to mistrust and being slighted. All of this leads to loss of effectiveness and efficiency because of the inevitable infighting among stakeholders.

Sabotaging relationships during initiating can be addressed several ways. It is first important to strive to develop and maintain a working relationship among stakeholders through open and honest dialogue not just between project managers and stakeholders but among stakeholders themselves. Second, if project managers see sabotage occurring, however subtle, they must raise the matter up the chain of command to at least make upper management aware that it is happening and to articulate its eventual impact to the project.

5.4.9 Not Engaging in Good Faith Negotiations

In a sense, all of the previous ethical situations and transgressions are examples of not negotiating in good faith. This one, however, is broader in the sense that it is the intent of the negotiation. The idea here is that not negotiating in good faith is trying to achieve a result through the use of unethical behavior (e.g., lying, stealing). Failure to negotiate in good faith (not the same as being gullible) has considerable consequences. Trust and communications break down, effectiveness and efficiency decline because no one trusts any results, regardless of scale, and verification and validation thus become the norm.

Not engaging in good faith negotiations can be addressed by doing the opposite: engaging in good faith negotiations. This is demonstrated by being open and honest about information with internal and external stakeholders. Of course, with external stakeholders, the interests of the company must still be protected.

5.5 PLANNING AND ETHICS

The significance of ethical issues during planning is that they can lead to poor and inaccurate reporting because the cost, schedule, and scope baselines are not realistic. Consequently, accurate and timely reporting will have the greatest impact (Table 5.2).

5.5.1 Padding

One of the most misunderstood ethical dilemmas is padding, which is augmenting an estimate to account for any unknowns. What most people do is confuse this one with adding a contingency, a calculated determination of a resource amount to deal with a certain contingency. Padding is random and usually across the board without much forethought;

TABLE 5.2

Planning and Ethics

	Compliance	Effectiveness	Accurate and Timely Information	Efficiency	Protection of Resources
Padding		√		√	
No accountability		√			√
Lying	√		√		
Allowing groupthink		√	√	√	
Using false information knowingly			√		
Providing unreliable cost and schedule baseline	√				
Not having a work breakdown structure		√	√	√	
Understating work effort		√	√	√	

contingency estimating is setting aside a specific amount of resources (e.g., time, money) to deal with a scenario should it occur.

Padding becomes an ethical dilemma because it provides an erroneous basis for calculating time and cost estimates and may mislead whoever is given a proposal. It also leads to artificially inflating estimates and may result in eventually overcharging the customer.

Perhaps the biggest consequences with padding is that it can lead to wastefully applying resources to activities that do not add much value while simultaneously taking resources away from those that add value to the customer. It can also mean that the customer overpays for some activities and underpays for others, thus creating waste.

Padding can be addressed in several ways. One way is to request that stakeholders estimate costs using statistically reliable estimating techniques, such as parametric and three-point estimating. Another way is to have in-depth reviews of all estimating assumptions done by team members to cross-check for bad estimates. Finally, estimating standards can be provided for certain categories of tasks, based on either historical records or industry standards.

5.5.2 No Accountability

Translated, no one is held responsible for delivering results. Instead, the project operates, as the U.S. Army says, as a chicken with its head cut off. Few people, if any, know who is to do what and when to deliver. Assumed roles, responsibilities, and authorities overlap. No one, it seems, is in charge or knows what is happening.

Naturally, the consequences are quite clear. No one is held responsible for achieving results; therefore, few will once the project goes into execution. Typically, meetings upon meetings pile up with no results and no end in sight. In addition, resources are squandered, perhaps even lost, even before the project moves into execution.

This ethical dilemma can be addressed by creating a responsibility matrix that reflects roles and responsibilities based on a solid work breakdown structure to ensure that the goals and objectives will be achieved once the project moves into execution.

5.5.3 Lying

This, as is initiating, is an ethical issue. Under no circumstance should it occur. Human nature, of course, deviates from this principle from time to time. During planning, lying can occur quite frequently, as might be suspected, especially as it relates to time and cost estimates. It is important to realize that poor estimating may not be the result of lying and, quite frankly, is often the case. Lying is a deliberate action to deceive and often it tied to other ethical issues like low-balling.

Lying has many consequences. From a planning standpoint, it results in allocating resources to incorrect priorities and can eventually delay the execution of a project in an effort to seek additional resources or reallocate them. Both cases lead to inefficiency and ineffectiveness.

Lying can be addressed using several tools and techniques. Each stakeholder's estimates can be cross-checked, assumptions made by estimators can be revisited, the results of projects of a similar nature can be reviewed, and outside experts can be brought in.

5.6 EXECUTING AND ETHICS

The significance of ethical dilemmas during executing is that they can lead to a project not following the baselines and, subsequently, getting out of control. Adhering to plans becomes more difficult as stakeholders fail to act as a team because each is likely following a different or misinterpreted vision and not performing according to plans. All ethical dilemmas are impacted (Table 5.3), though effectiveness is the hardest hit.

5.6.1 Mischarging

Mischarging is not uncommon and basically involves charging to the wrong account number for the work performed, which can cause all sorts of complications. Mischarging can result in a customer being charged for work that was never authorized, can cause accounting complications, and can possibly lead to legal issues, especially when it involves government contracts. Mischarging, when it happens accidentally, is not much of an issue because it can often be corrected; it becomes serious when it is blatant, persistent, and uncorrected. A company can face civil and criminal liability, and so can individuals.

Mischarging can be minimized in several ways. Start by ensuring that everyone knows exactly what the charge numbers are available to them and under what circumstances they are to be charged to. A periodic audit of charging practices can also be conducted to ensure compliance.

5.6.2 Misinformation or Disinformation

Information is one of the greatest resources of a project. When that information is tainted in some way, it can have undesirable consequences. Misinformation is spread unintentionally, and disinformation is spread intentionally; both are deliberately false. Regardless of the intent, when incorrect information is spread, it can affect the quality of decisions, hurt the ability to execute good decisions, cause rework, create confusion, and perhaps most importantly destroy trust among stakeholders.

Several actions can be taken to deal with misinformation and disinformation. Continuous communication among stakeholders can be encouraged, information used on the project can be verified and cross-checked, outside

TABLE 5.3

Executing and Ethics

	Compliance	Effectiveness	Accurate and Timely Information	Efficiency	Protection of Resources
Mischarging	√	√	√	√	
Misinformation or disinformation		√	√	√	
Straying from plan without authorization		√		√	
Violating confidentiality	√		√		√
Jeopardizing working relationships		√		√	
Vilifying peers		√			√
Violating employee rights	√	√			
Deliberately underperforming		√		√	
Squashing dissent		√	√		
Ignoring needs of team members		√		√	
Lacking reliable, consistent treatment of team members		√		√	
Not encouraging collaboration		√		√	
Dismissing without cause	√	√		√	
Sending a defective product to customer	√	√		√	
Unauthorized copying	√				√
Lacking consistent enforcement of standards	√	√		√	

opinions can be sought to verify information, and effective listening skills can be applied.

5.6.3 Straying from the Plan without Authorization

One of the quickest ways projects get into trouble is that they fail to follow their plan. Instead, a good plan is placed on a shelf, and the project goes on a different course. Sometimes this is by design; sometimes it is not. Regardless, to allow straying from a plan without authorization has several consequences. It can lead to scope creep, which is an unintended expansion of what the project was supposed to accomplish. It can also lead to rework to make up for work not done or to undo work. To allow straying from a plan is a violation of a promise to deliver according to expectations held by the customer.

Straying from plans without authorization can be prevented by ensuring good integrated change management processes and procedures are in place, reviewing periodically performance against the plan, publishing responsibilities identified in the plan, and simply referring to the plan throughout the execution of the project.

5.6.4 Violating Confidentiality

Whether in an organizational relationship (e.g., partnership) or in a person-to-person relationship, confidentiality is essentially for building trust and collaborating on a project. Violating confidentiality means not spreading entrusted data or information. If it occurs, the consequences can be quite apparent. People no longer share information, people are not invited to meetings, and politics become rampant. Sometimes all this can result in litigation for violating agreements and releasing proprietary information.

Violations of confidentiality can be avoided by stressing the importance of protecting proprietary information, instituting processes and procedures to prevent protected data and information from being released, and reporting to the appropriate organization or people when it occurs.

5.6.5 Jeopardizing Working Relationships

Collaboration is key among stakeholders if a project is to be completed successfully. An interdependent relationship among all stakeholders often exists. Occasionally, however, relationships go awry. Politics and personality differences, for example, interfere with this collaboration. The situation can deteriorate so much that people no longer want to work with each other. Some people deliberately do whatever they can to jeopardize relationships, and it is unfair to the other stakeholders to allow these actions to continue. Failure to address purposely jeopardizing working relationships has several consequences, including lowering team morale, decreasing productivity, and causing other people to assume an unreasonable workload.

To address this issue, people who purposely try to jeopardize working relationships can be confronted, the issue can be forced out in the open, and the parties involved can be influenced to resolve their differences. Greater team building can also be encouraged among tasks.

5.6.6 Violating Employee Rights

While there is plenty of talk of respecting employee rights, the reality is that quite often they are violated, particularly when an economy goes into a tailspin. The employer–employee relationship sometimes gets strained if the power relationship between the two gets altered. Once in awhile, someone in a position of authority can, either by design or by accident, abuse their position in such a way that violates employee rights. For example, this can also occur among peers as team members on a project, fearful of losing their jobs, pressure people to leave or ostracize them if one individual does not conform. Of course, under either scenario, this behavior can have several consequences. The pressure can inhibit discussion and participation, thereby reducing the overall effectiveness of the team. It can also lead to legal complications if the violation of right becomes too extreme.

Several actions can be taken to prevent the violation of employee rights. A concerted effort can be made to engage stakeholders in key discussion to encourage not only support but also a feeling of inclusion. The issue can be confronted right away when the violation occurs. The issue can then be taken to higher levels if it seems the ethical dilemma could lead to legal complications.

5.6.7 Vilifying Peers

Also known as character assassination, vilifying peers can lead to very bad working relationships. There are many ways people can impugn the character of an individual; some of it is direct, though more often it is indirect. An example of direct vilifying is sending out inflammatory e-mails or blatantly attacking a person's character during meetings. An example of indirect vilifying is spreading innuendos about someone. Vilifying peers is an ethical dilemma that can generate in demoralization of the project team, which impacts its productivity and overall effectiveness.

It is necessary to ensure that vilification is stopped at its source. Otherwise, the project will be imperiled; the problem is no one wants to admit to or to address vilification. It takes courage to take the step, but project managers need to call people who are doing this out as soon as possible. Some actions to take include going to the source of the vilification, bringing the parties involved together to resolve their differences, and agreeing to stop further character assassination. If necessary, elevate the issue to the company's human resources department or upper management team members if it becomes intolerable to the victim.

5.6.8 Deliberately Underperforming

Underperforming for the sole purpose of negatively impacting a project is an ethical dilemma for the simple reason that value is not being delivered to the project. More money is going out than is coming in as a result. People deliberately underperform for several reasons. They were unhappy being assigned to the project in the first place, they do not like the project manager or some of the other team members, they believe the project is doomed to failure, or they see the project as a stepping stone to a better position or project.

Failure to deal with someone who is underperforming can have harmful effects on a project. It can negatively affect the pace or momentum of the project, can cause others to unfairly assume more of the workload, can result in rework, and can lead to increased overhead costs.

Several actions can be taken to deal with stakeholders who are deliberately underperforming. A request can be made that the person be removed from the team, the person can be given responsibilities that have a minor influence on the outcome of the project, the person can be teamed with another who is a hard charger to induce the former to produce, and peer pressure can be applied by showcasing the performance of others and the lack of the person's performance.

5.6.9 Squashing Dissent

This is an ethical dilemma because it violates individuals' right to be honest about their performance on a project or, indeed, its overall performance. On some projects, even the best performing ones, team members experience groupthink, in which they suppress differences of opinion, acquire a feeling of superiority, even invincibility, and have the illusion, even deniability, of reality. Team members think the team is effective, but in reality it may not be very effective at all because it filters out information that may be necessary to adapt to changing circumstances. It also inhibits the accurate dissemination and reporting of information.

Several actions can be taken to offset the danger of squashing dissent. New people can be brought onboard to provide fresh insight on issues and challenges. External consultants can be sought for a fresh opinion. Stakeholders who were ringleaders and who have contributed to groupthink can be removed. An adversarial stance can be taken by the project manager on key issues, challenges, and concerns just to shake up people's thinking.

5.6.10 Ignoring Needs of Team Members

Project managers are responsible for satisfying the needs of stakeholders, including members of their team. Stakeholders have a wide range of needs of which project managers need to be aware if they hope to motivate them in a way that increases their performance. It becomes an ethical dilemma if their needs are deliberately ignored when it comes to getting the job done. Since project managers are responsible for the overall performance of the team, they need to find out what those needs are and try to satisfy them with the means under their control. To do otherwise is not taking responsibility for the overall performance of the team. Obviously, failure to address those needs will impact both the efficiency and effectiveness of both the individual and the overall team.

This ethical dilemma can be addressed by maintaining an ongoing dialogue with each team member, keeping team members posted regarding the status of their requests, finding alternative ways to develop at least an interim solution to help fulfill their needs, and, if money or time is in short supply, performing a cost–benefit analysis and asking for more money or time or coming up with a more effective way to complete the project.

5.6.11 Lacking Reliable, Consistent Treatment of Team Members

On many teams, not everyone is equal; some team members will rise to a position of superiority relative to the others. Often, they will receive preferential treatment while others are left with little or no influence. Social scientists refer to this as the iron law of oligarchy. Unfortunately, this iron law can get so extreme that it ends up demoralizing some team members. A project manager can fall into the trap of supporting a few and disregarding the others. The implications are clear with this sort of behavior. Some people will tune out by keeping silent and not participating; some will do what they can to sabotage any progress; still others, oftentimes the most skillful, will depart. This, as might be suspected, affects the efficiency and effectiveness of the team in a negative way.

Several actions can be taken to prevent this ethical dilemma from arising. Everyone at meetings should at least be asked for their insights or opinions. Key assignments can be rotated to ensure that everyone has the opportunity to participate in the project's outcome. People can be teamed up with some of the perceived favorites to share the visibility.

5.6.12 Not Encouraging Collaboration

While at first this might not seem like an ethical issue, it is. If the project manager or any team members deliberately encourage divisiveness for personal gain, the emphasis is on personal needs and not that of the project. A project that is efficient and effective requires the collaboration of all stakeholders. A project manager needs to make collaboration a top priority; otherwise, the project will not operate at peak levels. Failure to collaborate, therefore, can impact a project by reducing the payback for every dollar invested that does not meet the goals and objectives of the project. In addition, it could lead to infighting and negative competition.

Collaboration can be encouraged by implementing greater team-building activities and events. Successful collaborative events can be rewarded in addition to individual achievements. Another approach is greater sharing of information and team participation in resolving ethical dilemmas, such as brainstorming.

5.6.13 Dismissing without Cause

Removing a team member may make sense for the good of the team, but it is necessary to have a cause for doing so other than disagreeing with a person's style. Frequently, personality differences lead to this dilemma, but this does not warrant their dismissal unless the differences are so pronounced that the project suffers. If people are removed from a project because of personality or viewpoint differences, it can have negative impacts, such as creating an atmosphere of groupthink, not acquiring innovative ideas to further the progress of a project, and losing potentially valuable expertise and knowledge. Project managers who dismiss without cause are committing an ethical violation because they are making such decisions not in the interests of their projects but for their own comfort. They could also set themselves up for being embroiled in legal complications.

To dismiss a team member in an ethical manner, facts and data must be used. A good faith effort must also be made to resolve differences first using conflict management skills.

5.6.14 Sending a Defective Product to a Customer

Although rarely done on purpose, knowingly sending a defective product to a customer is clearly an unethical issue. Essentially, expectations were not met, and the team is trying to abdicate responsibility. Actions exemplifying this unethical behavior include circumventing testing standards, purposely letting the sustaining and maintenance portion of the product life cycle absorb the costs of poor work, and putting the parent organizations and stakeholder reputations at risk. This is a failure of due diligence and due care, which could lead to potential legal complications related to compliance with laws and regulations.

Several actions can be taken to avoid sending a defective product to the customer. Standards and guidelines and testing processes can be adhered to, metrics on defects can be published, and quality tools and techniques (e.g., Ishikawa diagramming, Pareto charts) can be used.

5.6.15 Unauthorized Copying

Violation of copyright laws is serious business, although it is often difficult to prove and can be costly to win a case. In some cases, however, it can be rather obvious. Unauthorized copying is not restricted to the printed word; it covers other areas such as drawings and software. It can also get complicated when working on a joint venture and dealing with intellectual property. Obviously, the biggest impact to a project is the failure to comply with the copyright laws; there is also the threat of civil and criminal litigation by failing to protect either the organization's or a partner's assets.

Copyright laws can be followed by ensuring everyone is aware of what is and is not permissible under them. People can also cross-check each other's work, thereby increasing the likelihood of detecting any violations.

5.6.16 Lacking Consistent Enforcement of Standards

Everyone should follow the same standards on a project team. If exceptions are made, then one of them will likely, ironically, be the rule. Standards enable everyone to work together and more often than not reduce duplication of effort. Unfortunately, requiring consistent enforcement of standards can be difficult because sometimes team members like to put their personal stamp on the work. This situation makes it difficult to sustain or maintain the deliverable in the future and for team members to work collaboratively in achieving the goals and objectives of the project. In standards related to topics like safety, it can also result in lack of compliance with laws and regulations.

Several things can be done to ensure better consistent enforcement of standards. The project manager can model the standards personally, can communicate the standards, and can require review and testing according to the standards to include publishing metrics on failure to comply with standards.

5.7 MONITORING AND CONTROLLING AND ETHICS

The significance of ethical dilemmas during monitoring and controlling is that it becomes difficult to ascertain how the project is progressing according to plan. The reason is that the information is unreliable and inaccurate. The impact of many of these ethical issues may be compounded by ethical dilemmas arising during the other project management processes (e.g., initiating, planning) (Table 5.4).

5.7.1 Misreporting

Intentionally not reporting accurate information about the performance of the project is an ethical issue and transgression and can occur for many

TABLE 5.4

Monitoring and Controlling and Ethics

	Compliance	Effectiveness	Accurate and Timely Information	Efficiency	Protection of Resources
Misreporting (underreporting or overreporting)	√		√		
Deliberately withholding bad news	√		√		
Inflating expense reports	√		√	√	√
Mischarging	√		√	√	√
Destroying or stealing vital information	√		√		√
Massaging or not sharing information with critical stakeholders	√		√		
Not using reliable data to generate information			√		
Not using plans to report progress	√		√	√	

reasons. The project manager or other key stakeholder may misreport to avoid embarrassment or negative ramifications for themselves and the parent organization. It may occur because of the desire to receive an award, such as an award fee if applicable, from the customer. Team members may figure that the misreporting will be compensated for in anticipated future performance, thereby making it a nonissue. Whatever the reason, misreporting has severe consequences. It can lead to legal issues with key stakeholders, such as shareholders using financial legislation to seek redress. It can also lead to management making poor decisions that only further complicate a project's troubles.

The likelihood of misreporting can be removed by validating the data used to generate reports, establishing ongoing, consistent reporting on progress to key stakeholders, and distributing reports to key stakeholders, such as steering committee members, who ask questions regarding the meaning behind the content of the reports.

5.7.2 Massaging or Not Sharing Information with Critical Stakeholders

In a project environment, reliable information is critical for making important decisions by key stakeholders. Without critical information some key stakeholders can make decisions that can negatively affect the outcome of a project. This can result in a company becoming legally liable for not demonstrating due diligence in its reporting because the information presented does not portray an accurate view.

Sometimes, key information is not delivered to key stakeholders or is massaged in such a way that the stakeholders fail to ascertain the information's significance. It could be due to politics, fear (e.g., shoot the messenger), or just neglectfulness on the part of people preparing, for example, a report containing the information.

This situation becomes an ethical issue if the intent is to purposely keep certain key stakeholders in the dark or to fulfill some nefarious purpose, such as making political gains or avoiding reality in the hope that the situation will go away.

This ethical situation can be prevented by developing a communications management plan and following it, developing a standard set of reports that are produced and distributed regularly, and inviting key stakeholders to participate in the affairs of the project. A periodic project review can also be requested in which the results are communicated up the chain of command.

5.7.3 Not Using Reliable Data to Generate Information

Data by itself have no meaning; data coupled with meaning to serve a purpose are called information. All information, therefore, depends on data, and the quality of the latter affects the quality of the former. Information, in turn, supports decision making, and bad data lead to bad information, which may lead to bad decision making because the content lacks accuracy.

It becomes an ethical dilemma when project team members carelessly generate data that will be used to create information for decision makers. They have violated the trust bestowed upon them by key stakeholders to provide reliable data. These stakeholders include not only the project manager or sponsor but also other members of senior management and shareholders.

Not using reliable data to generate information can be avoided by scrubbing, or cleansing, data before they are used to generate information, verifying data for validity and reliability, and conducting walkthroughs or peer reviews of reports prior to their release.

5.7.4 Not Using Plans to Report Progress

Amazingly, many project managers and their team go through major efforts to develop comprehensive plans and then execute the project without ever using the plans as a road map. As a consequence, team members run around helter-skelter, resources are expended needlessly on rework to fix defects, and tension runs high as finger-pointing often becomes the norm. All of this leads to waste.

This has ethical consequences for several reasons. If the plans were presented to a steering team for approval and then the team takes a different direction from what was approved, the team is disingenuous because it deviates from what was promised. Also, reporting on progress may be based on conjecture or even deliberate misleading to key stakeholders, from senior management to shareholders.

This ethical issue can be appropriately dealt with by using all baselines (e.g., schedule, cost, scope) to track performance, conducting ongoing status review meetings to discuss performance to those baselines, or sending fact-based reports to key stakeholders on a regular basis.

5.7.5 Deliberately Not Reporting Bad News

This one is tied closely with misreporting. In this situation, reporting becomes very selective. Only the good news is reported all the time. Experienced project managers know that few, if any, projects go smoothly. Yet, occasionally, a project manager reports that everything is going perfectly well: Cost, schedule, and technical performance are all in the green.

Then, at the last minute the project fails to deliver. Such behavior puts a company at risk with authorities as well as causes decision makers to make poor decisions.

There are ethical concerns here. The information portrayed by the project manager is clearly an attempt to deceive for many reasons, often for advancement or fear. Often there is an attitude that perception is reality; this is obviously false when the schedule begins to slide, the costs start to escalate, and rework becomes the norm. Then, if it is a big project that can impact investors, it can lead to legal issues.

Several steps can be taken to ensure that balanced reporting occurs on a project. Certain stakeholders should review reports prior to their release. Metrics should be established based on reliable data to be a major element in the reports; facts and data are more often than not good antidotes to poor reporting. All facts, data, and assumptions that provide information for the reports should be challenged.

5.7.6 Inflating Expense Reports

Managing against a cost baseline is obviously very critical to a project's success. Few projects exist where money is no object. Unfortunately, some people take advantage of a project, especially when it involves travel. If the expense reports are not scrutinized carefully, then costs can easily escalate and could actually lead to legal issues because customers are billed for expenses that should never have happened. These reports, too, often contain erroneous or unclear information and, a clear warning sign, are submitted late in the hopes that they will be approved without being examined with a pile of other expense reports.

The inflation of expense reports can be prevented, as much as possible, by setting a limit on costs for travel and training, reviewing certain expenses that exceed a certain threshold, assigning someone on the team to review all expense reports prior to approval, and setting standards for what is and is not permissible. Ideally, someone independent to the project should perform this function, which is not always possible in a small or even medium-size firm.

5.7.7 Destroying or Stealing Vital Information

Data and information are the property of the organization and not the individuals working on the team. Some people think that just because they created or developed information they own it. In reality, the parent organization owns it in exchange for a salary or a work-for-hire agreement. Destroying or stealing vital information can result in legal complexities, especially if it violates confidentiality agreements regarding proprietary information. It can cause the project to fail because of a loss of important information used when creating deliverables. It also violates the trust that the organization gives individuals to protect its resources.

It is pretty clear that destroying or stealing vital issues is an ethical issue. Any theft of company information or other resources or their wanton destruction, however perceived justified by an individual, is an ethical violation of trust.

Attempts can be made to reduce the impact of this ethical dilemma, but it is difficult to prevent. If a person is determined to do it, only its impact can be minimized by, for example, making backups of information, reporting any suspected activity related to this dilemma, and securing vital information by restricting access to it.

5.8 CLOSING AND ETHICS

The significance of ethical dilemmas during closing is that they can lead to litigation, reputational damage, and poor customer satisfaction. All ethical areas are impacted (Table 5.5), although effectiveness is the hardest hit.

TABLE 5.5

Closing and Ethics

	Compliance	Effectiveness	Accurate and Timely Information	Efficiency	Protection of Resources
Not delivering results as promised		√			√
Not satisfying contractual requirements	√	√		√	
Falsifying records	√		√		√

5.8.1 Not Delivering Results as Promised

It is one thing to not deliver as promised due to some technical difficulty on a project; it is another to not deliver while all along giving the impression that expectations will be met at the conclusion of a project. Dashed expectations under the latter are a genuine effort to mislead key stakeholders. The project, for which it exists in the first place, not only becomes a waste of money but also does not add any value to the organization.

To a large extent, not delivering results under such circumstances is coupled with other ethical dilemmas, such as lying and deliberately not reporting bad news. Throughout the entire life cycle of such a project few, if any, project management disciplines and information are available for performance. In a sense, such projects operate under the radar until the last minute, leaving key stakeholders with dashed expectations. Of course, the key stakeholders need to be continuously vigilant about all projects, but once in awhile, particularly in large organizations, some projects operate for quite some time under the radar until it is too late for key stakeholders, such as shareholders.

This ethical dilemma can be avoided by developing a standard set of reports (known as a report deck) that is replete with important metrics. You can then distribute the report deck on a regular basis to key stakeholders. If the project is big enough, a steering committee should also be established and special effort should be made to keep them engaged.

5.8.2 Not Satisfying Contractual Requirements

This one is closely tied to the last one but is more focused on the terms and conditions of the contract. The project comes down to the end, and then the project manager reveals that certain terms and conditions will not be met. In this case, the major expectations overall may be met, but there are certain terms and conditions that were overlooked intentionally during the contract. Now the customer has no other choice but to yield to accept the product simply because it needs the product, for example, to obtain competitive advantage in the marketplace. If the project manager has not kept the sponsor or customer apprised throughout the project life cycle with the intent to mislead, it becomes an ethical dilemma that can lead to litigation and higher sustaining and maintenance cost later.

This ethical dilemma can be prevented by engaging the customer and the sponsor on the project to one extent or another, keeping them apprised of progress on a regular basis, and continually comparing performance with contractual requirements.

5.8.3 Falsifying Records

Occasionally, to cover up mistakes or to disguise their failure to perform their responsibilities, someone will falsify records. This may happen when fees for performance are distributed during and at the conclusion of a project. The hope is often that if the project winds down and the customer is happy then the likelihood of getting caught diminishes unless, of course, an audit occurs. Not only can this lead to legal issues, but it also can result in bad reporting and reflect a potential misuse of resources.

The potential for falsifying records can be offset by requiring an audit trail of all project activities, conducting periodic reviews of project documentation, and calling for an external review of all project documentation from an independent organization.

5.9 GENERAL ETHICAL DILEMMAS

The following list of ethical dilemmas is meant to be an overview of some of the ones that can occur throughout the entire life cycle of a project or during each of the major processes of initiating, planning, executing, monitoring and controlling, and closing. For simplification they have been grouped into one or more groups and, as before, can overlap with some of the others. The four groups are (1) people, or human resources; (2) process, or adherence to policies, procedures, laws, and regulations; (3) performance, or implementing the project; and (4) perception, or how actions are perceived by others external to the project.

5.9.1 People and Ethics

These ethical dilemmas are the most pervasive simply because they deal substantially with the people side of project management. They are more challenging and complex to resolve. They span across all five ethical categories and throughout all the project management processes and phases (Table 5.6).

TABLE 5.6

People and Ethics

	Compliance	Effectiveness	Accurate and Timely Information	Efficiency	Protection of Resources
Allowing a toxic culture to exist	√	√	√	√	√
Incivility		√		√	
Harassment	√	√		√	√
Violation of privacy	√				
Retaliation	√	√		√	√
Coercion	√	√		√	√
Not respecting values		√		√	
Not providing honest feedback	√		√		
Treating people inequitably		√		√	
Lacking personal responsibility		√		√	
Spreading malicious rumors		√	√	√	
Misusing power and position	√		√		√
Discriminating	√	√	√	√	√
Encouraging or not dealing with infighting		√	√	√	√
Not treating everyone fairly and respectfully		√		√	
Not stopping hidden agendas		√	√	√	
Exploiting people		√		√	√
Deliberately and maliciously damaging reputations	√				√

5.9.1.1 Allowing a Toxic Culture to Exist

The atmosphere of a project often reflects the tone set by the overall organization. If the overall atmosphere is negative, then it will permeate the project. Such an atmosphere can affect all aspects of a project from the way it does business to how it respects or reacts to given situations. Productivity, use of resources, and information quality all can lead to rework if affected. In some cases, the toxic culture can cause people to act in such a way that can legally put them and the greater organization at risk. It is an ethical dilemma because it can set a tone that encourages people to behave in ways that are unacceptable under normal circumstances.

About the best project managers can do in this situation is to adapt to the environment and follow their own ethical standards. The pressure can be immense, especially if people feel they are trapped and have to do what is necessary to survive. Project managers should follow their own conscience and protect the team as much as possible to execute the project in the most effective and efficient manner possible.

5.9.1.2 Incivility

This involves how individuals treat those around them. It has much to do with how people are perceived on a project. Incivility can also exist among peers. Peers may elect to treat an individual or group of people with disrespect, based on race, religion, sex, ethnicity, and even personality. Incivility toward individuals will impact their performance in terms of achieving the goals and objectives of the project and also by lowering morale. It is an ethical dilemma because it affects the dignity and self-respect of individuals.

Several actions can be taken to offset the ethical dilemma of incivility. Tasks can be assigned to prevent people who are uncivil toward each other from working together. The source of the problem can be addressed by having an open discussion to get the individuals to resolve their differences. Individuals can be removed from the project. People can be required to take training courses on diversity, which covers everything from physical characteristic to thinking styles.

5.9.1.3 Harassment

This is an obvious example of an ethical dilemma. The point can be further expanded to include harassment in general, which goes beyond the sexual dimension. Harassment can take the form of bullying on the job or verbal assault by a leader or a peer. It can impede a person's ability to achieve the goals and objectives of the project as well as hinder optimum performance. Allowed to be taken to the extreme, harassment can lead to legal complications. It is an ethical dilemma because no one should come to work and experience a threatening environment.

Project managers can address this problem by analyzing their approach toward managing their project and by making changes to their management style if necessary. It should be given attention early on if witnessed among stakeholders, and help should be sought from human resources or some other organization to intervene to discontinue the behavior.

5.9.1.4 Violation of Privacy

The right to privacy in the workplace is a very difficult dilemma in trying to determine when the rights of an organization can impact the rights of an individual. In some cases, the former has precedence over the latter, and vice versa. With computing technology and cell phones increasingly being used in the workplace, the line between organizations and individuals can be complicated despite the fact that the courts have generally ruled that there is a right to privacy. For instance, if team members believe their right to privacy has been violated, it can affect their efficiency and the effectiveness of their performance; it can also get the lawyers involved. It is an ethical dilemma because it affects individuals' rights.

It is necessary to at least be conscious of this dynamic tension between the rights of the organization and the rights of the individual. If there is a question over the right to privacy, it is essential to find out the circumstances and the policies and procedures that should be followed and to seek assistance from human resources on how to handle the situation.

5.9.1.5 Retaliation

Again, this one is very sensitive legally. A person may report that the project is in trouble or that something else is occurring unethically on the project. Management or peers may seek to retaliate against the individual, resulting in a host of legal and nonlegal problems. Whistle-blowers frequently face this problem in overt and subtle ways.

Project managers may not even be privy to the fact that the individual has filed a complaint, especially if the person goes through a hotline investigation. If they are, however, they need to report any retaliation that occurs. Of course, it goes without saying that they should avoid retaliating against an individual.

5.9.1.6 Coercion

Power comes in many forms, such as by virtue of position or personality. Using power to get people to do something, especially something illegal or unethical, that they would not ordinarily do is treading on dangerous territory. Not only will it invite a person to seek payback, but it can also result in a person not wanting to participate later on the project and can lead to legal complications. It is an ethical issue because it violates the dignity of the individual.

Project managers should seek to influence behavior in a way that does not require coercion. Sometimes, pressure needs to be exerted to achieve results, but that does not mean they should be threatened in a way that violates their free will. Ways to avoid coercion is to apply participative management on the project, to engender accountability for results through the definition of roles, accountabilities, and authorities, and to construct responsibility assignment matrices.

5.9.1.7 No Respect for Values

This dilemma covers the values of the organization, the project, and the individual. All people have a set of culturally based values that help them to guide their lives. In a world of global projects, respecting values of other countries, organizations, and individuals is critical to getting people to perform efficiently and to achieve the goals and objectives of the project. Failure to respect these values can affect the overall performance of a project as well as alienate people. It is an ethical dilemma because it affects the dignity of the individual.

A special effort needs to be made to respect the different cultural values that exist in the project environment. The project manager may not agree with them but, unless they harm individuals, has an ethical obligation to respect them.

5.9.1.8 No Provision of Honest Feedback

A less polite way of describing this is lying. Honesty is the best way to preserve credibility, and once a person loses that credibility it becomes next to impossible to regain it. Lying can occur in all life cycles, but it is most likely to arise during initiating and monitoring and controlling. However, at no time should it be allowed.

Project managers should set an example by not lying of course; they also need to confront it when others lie. They can help minimize the chance of lying by collecting and publishing reliable and frequent metrics about the performance of your project. They can also question remarks and assumptions made by individuals rather than allowing people to continue lying. This becomes even more challenging when a key, powerful stakeholder continues to lie, and everyone else knows otherwise.

5.9.1.9 Treat People Inequitably

People by their very nature will give preference to others for all sorts of reasons. They like their personality. They have the same heritage. They have the same physical characteristics. The challenge is when it interferes with treating people the same despite the differences. It can affect *esprit de corps*, causing people to underperform because they do not feel included. Individuals who feel they are treated inequitably will soon disengage themselves from the project, if not physically then mentally and emotionally. It becomes an ethical issue because it is not employing resources as they were intended by the organization.

Project managers can prevent treating people inequitably by ensuring that everyone on the project has an opportunity to have a say in its direction and to participate in achieving its outcome. Tasks and responsibilities also can be assigned that will encourage people to work together to develop deliverables.

5.9.1.10 Lack of Personal Responsibility

Everyone associated with the project should have a sense of personal responsibility for their share of work that contributes to the overall success of the project. Unfortunately, sometimes some individuals accept responsibility for results that go well, and when things do not go well they shift the blame to someone else. If accepting a lack of responsibility prevails on a project, then it is likely to head toward disaster. People need to accept responsibility if for no other reason but to have a sense of ownership in the project.

People can be encouraged to accept results by offering opportunities to participate in the planning and execution of the project, assigning roles and responsibilities clearly, and following up on actions to occur now and in the future.

5.9.1.11 Spread of Malicious Rumors

Unsubstantiated rumors, especially negative ones, really serve no purpose. The negative ones can be especially devastating to the morale and productivity of a project. These negative rumors span everything from being outsourced to being forced to working overtime without compensation (depending on employment status, of course). Negative rumors serve no purpose other than to focus people's minds on nonproductive work. Some rumors can be downright malicious in nature, impugning the reputation of an individual or an entire project team. The ethical consequences can be immense because they are not above the waterline and are difficult to address.

It is difficult to counter rumors because it is not easy to find the originator of the rumor and try to follow up on it. The best way to deal with rumors is to hold meetings with key stakeholders to confront them on the merits of the rumor and then to communicate their responses to the team. Facts and data can also be collected that either substantiate or counter the rumor and then the findings communicated. The important action is to address the rumor before it has harmful effects on the project.

5.9.1.12 Misuse of Power and Position

Power and position often go together, although in some cases they can be separate. When together they entice some people to allow themselves to be consumed by both. Project managers, while often not formal agents of an organization, can have power that spans the entire continuum from weak to strong, depending on the organizational structure of the parent organization. A person's power, if strong and left unchecked, can lead to abuse of certain team members. This one has obvious ethical issues surrounding it. If project managers violate the rights of individuals they can land themselves and the organization in court. If they use power to influence reporting, then the information may provide an inaccurate view of what is happening. If they have too much power, project managers can misuse resources for personal use.

Project managers need to question whether they are violating the power and authority entrusted to them. The arrogance of power can be avoided by obtaining participation by key stakeholders throughout the life of a project and asking stakeholders for continuous feedback on performance.

5.9.1.13 Discrimination

Discrimination takes many forms, including age, height, color, and ethnicity. Despite all the laws and training on diversity, it continues without abatement. Just because individuals claim they do not discriminate does not mean they do not practice discrimination. To a large extent, learning not to discriminate is a combination of knowledge and awareness. Discrimination can be quite blatant, such as directly refusing to work with someone of a certain ethnicity, or subtle, such as deliberately not inviting someone to a project meeting because of their religion.

Discrimination by team members is serious business and happens more often than people might think. Discrimination should be addressed up front, not only because it is wrong and can have legal implications but also because it can kill team work, making the team less effective and efficient. It also allows the project's most valuable resource, people, to be abused.

Discrimination can be prevented by encouraging greater team member interaction, which in turn fosters greater sharing of emotion and discussion among different people. Diversity training can be offered. If it is a global project, people can be persuaded to learn about the culture of other people's projects.

5.9.1.14 Encourage or Not Deal with Infighting

Divide and conquer is a common technique used in political and military environments. Encouraging and tolerating infighting is also common in the project environment. The larger the project in terms of stakeholders, generally the more chance there is for infighting to become quite common. Naturally, infighting, not to be confused with competition, can be quite counterproductive. Goals and objectives can slip because of it;

rework can become the norm. Some team members find themselves so intimidated that they tune out and may not stop producing but no longer provide information.

Tolerating infighting is an ethical dilemma because it can lead to performing unethical actions. One side does things, such as spread malicious lies or fails to deliver, in an effort to sabotage the other side. If project managers engage in the infighting, it also demonstrates their reluctance to encourage collaboration to achieve a common goal as well as destroys their credibility.

Infighting can be dealt with by first maintaining independence and credibility through not engaging in the infighting. The fighters can be encouraged to resolve their differences by applying conflict management and team-building exercises. If anything, the issue can be elevated to superiors.

5.9.1.15 Not Treat Everyone Fairly and Equitably

In social science there is the law of oligarchy, meaning that in every group a core team of elites will form. In time, these people receive most of the rewards and other benefits, while the rest share a lesser amount. In other words, they become more equal than others and receive preferential treatment. This circumstance can have a negative impact on members of the team who are not part of the oligarchy, especially if the lion's share of the perks goes to a small group of preferred people who do not deserve it; they may be less attentive to their work, resulting in rework, and may not bother to direct their energies to achieve the goals and objectives of the project.

People can be treated more equitably and fairly by giving them a fair opportunity to participate on the project by asking for volunteers. Everyone can be given a chance for exposure to other key stakeholders by allowing them to give presentations about some aspect of the project.

5.9.1.16 Not Stopping Hidden Agendas

This dilemma is difficult to identify and work on because by its very nature it is hard to uncover. Often hidden agendas manifest themselves by a person's behavior that is exhibited negatively, such as disparaging comments about the process, certain people, and the quality of output, but it is done in such a way that the attack is indirect. Needless to say, this behavior can lower morale and cause a project to become stale, resulting in rework and not meeting goals and objectives in a timely manner. Information often appears confusing because it is difficult to ascertain what is true and what is false. It becomes an ethical issue if it is allowed to persist because people may operate on false information.

Hidden agendas can be addressed in several ways. The agendas can be called out in a meeting to uncover them and have others verify or discredit the person's exposed agenda. A private meeting can be held with the person to try to come up with a mutual resolution. The person can be removed from the project, thereby eliminating the hidden agenda.

5.9.1.17 Exploit People

Taking advantage of people for personal gain is wrong. Project managers who use people to gain the upper hand and take credit while not recognizing others is called exploitation. It is not the same as employing people to achieve the goals and objectives of the project, in which the focus is on the greater good. Exploiting simply misuses people, which in the end lowers performance and creates waste. It is unethical because in this case project managers put themselves first and the project second.

Project managers can overcome the temptation to exploit people and encourage others to do the same by always making decisions in the context of achieving the goals and objectives of the project, reemphasizing the vision of the project at meetings, and always asking what is in the best interests of the project whenever conflict or an issue arises.

5.9.1.18 Deliberate Malicious Damage to Reputations

People who feel animosity or jealousy toward another person sometimes exhibit it by trashing the reputations of the individuals; they can do the same for organizations and projects. When these people do that, and sometimes they may have a legitimate reason to do so, they harm not only the person, project, or organization but also themselves. If the malicious damage goes too far, then it can result in legal complications.

Malicious damage to reputations needs to be taken on when it occurs. Not doing anything can be construed as acceptance or even concurrence. It can be dealt with by addressing the comments up front with the individual or even at a team meeting. Human resources can also get involved if it appears that the malicious damage has the potential to become a legal issue.

TABLE 5.7

Process and Ethics

	Compliance	Effectiveness	Accurate and Timely Information	Efficiency	Protection of Resources
Receiving inappropriate entertainment and gifts	√				√
Conflict of interest relationship with customers and suppliers	√				
Lacking due diligence and due care	√				
Lacking objectivity and independence			√		
Massaging feedback			√		
Unequal access to information and other key resources		√	√	√	
Engaging in illicit activities	√				
Not reporting unethical behavior	√				

5.9.2 Process and Ethics

These ethical dilemmas affect primarily the ethical areas of compliance and accurate and timely information (Table 5.7). Many of them require making objective decisions, a difficult act to perform when judgment may be impaired without realizing it through the use of rationalization.

5.9.2.1 Receiving Inappropriate Entertainment and Gifts

While common sense would tell people that this one involves ethical dilemmas, it happens all too often. Some individuals will receive gifts and entertainment as if in denial that it can hinder their objectivity and independence in making a decision or that no one really cares. Frequently, the ethical situation deteriorates or the transgression increases to the point that obvious action has to be taken; otherwise the project and the organization will see a negative impact on resources used on the project and lawyers start getting involved. In some cases, attempts are made to cover up the fact that this situation is occurring, which only leads to commission of further ethical situations and transgressions.

There are limited options for dealing with this situation. The standard can be set by not receiving inappropriate entertainment and gifts. Even the mere appearance of this ethical dilemma can cause harm; therefore, the standard can be set by avoiding any direct or indirect implication by stepping away. If it is a procurement organization, let it deal with vendors or suppliers during the negotiation process. As for people on the team, a process should be set up for reviewing all receipts. Of course, if something is happening after hours and the project manager suspects it, he or she can contact human resources or call a hotline if one exists.

5.9.2.2 Conflict of Interest with Vendors and Suppliers

This one is related to the previous ethical dilemma, except it is direct. The stakeholders may have investments or have worked previously with a vendor or supplier and have assets with them. As with the previous one, this ethical situation can cloud individuals' judgment whether they realize it or not. Even the mere appearance can cause problems. And like the previous one, it can lead to serious legal complications.

Project managers, of course, should extricate themselves from any circumstance that may be construed, directly or indirectly, as a conflict of interest. They should expect others on their team to do the same. Human resources should be contacted, or suspicions should be called in to a hotline if one exists.

5.9.2.3 Lacking Due Diligence and Due Care

Due diligence involves investigating the facts and data to confirm or disconfirm the existence of processes and procedures in an organization. From a project management perspective, in the context of this book, it is verifying that the key principles, tools, and techniques are implemented on a project. For example, the project has a charter, a work breakdown structure, schedule, and cost baselines. A failure to have such disciplines, tools, and techniques is representative of a lack of due diligence. Lack of due care is the follow-through in the implementation of such techniques, tools, and disciplines on a project. It is their actual application under what constitutes being reasonable under a given set of circumstances.

Sometimes, no due diligence exists. Sometimes due diligence exists but not due care. Of course, if no due diligence exists then there is likely no due care; the former can exist without the latter but not vice versa. In an age of litigation, the safe bet is to have both in place, especially with a project that can impact the financial existence of the firm and shareholders are watching it closely. Exercising due diligence without due care is an ethical situation or transgression because it misleads key decision makers in thinking that what was said is actually what will be done.

Several steps can be taken to ensure due diligence and due care. Project management processes and deliverables can be developed as advocated by professional institutions. The discipline on the project is then exercised to ensure that the processes and deliverables are actually realized throughout the life cycle of a project.

5.9.2.4 Massaging Feedback

This dilemma involves posturing information in such a way that, when it is presented, it communicates a message that seems innocuous, when in fact the situation may be far worse than anyone realized. For example, some companies use a color code for status, such as red, green, and yellow for either one or more of the following categories: cost, schedule, quality, and risk. Amazingly, some project managers may be red in all categories, but when they give a summary report they report themselves as green. If they want to hedge their bets, they will report themselves as yellow. On large organizations and projects, this circumstance is quite common, especially when the number of reviewers increases. Project managers and other key stakeholders who massage feedback are doing themselves and key decision makers a disservice. They are not communicating an accurate portrayal on the status of their projects, which can lead to bad decisions as well as a lack of credibility.

Massaging of information can be prevented in several ways. If the project is not highly proprietary, everyone can be given free access to data about the project. Stakeholders, especially outside experts, can review for validity and reliability, the quality of the data, and the information for reports. High personal and professional standards can be exercised, and the status of the project can be reported on accurately.

5.9.2.5 Unequal Access to Key Information and Other Resources

Although most project management experts advocate the open sharing of information and other resources among team members and other stakeholders to get the job done, what often happens is that the iron law of oligarchy goes into effect. A few people have access to the resources (e.g., people, information, equipment, supplies), and the others find themselves searching and going without what they need. The result is people often wasting their time and effort by doing their work in a way that could have been done more efficiently if they had the resources to do their job. They may also have to perform rework, failing to achieve what they need, or having other people do their work. They may even lack reliable information to do their job because no one shared information about what they needed to know.

All project resources can be reviewed, and processes and procedures can be set up for people to access the resources that they need. If certain resources need to be managed or controlled, then these processes and procedures should be shared with everyone on the project—communicated to everyone instead of everyone operating out of ignorance. Common work areas can be constructed that enable people to access what they need to do their job. If people work virtually, they should have a single point of contact to get what they need to do their job.

5.9.2.6 Engaging in Illicit Activities

This dilemma involves activities like embezzlement, industrial espionage, etc. which, for most people, are construed as unethical. They entail serious violation of laws and regulations as well as not following policies and procedures. They can also involve any stakeholder on a project.

Such ethical dilemmas cannot be prevented from happening, but it can be ensured that all activities on the project comply with relevant organizational policies and procedures as well as laws and regulations. Of course, if anyone on the project becomes aware of the potential or real occurrence of illicit activities, report it immediately to the appropriate channels offered within the company or to the government if necessary.

5.9.2.7 Not Reporting Unethical Behavior

Doing nothing when witnessing something that is not right is fundamentally wrong; a person becomes complicit with the wrongful behavior whether or not they realize it. On a project, an unethical activity, especially one of wrongful intent, must be addressed—despite the consequences. While many people agree with that statement, a much fewer number of people actually exercise that notion. If the opposite existed, there would likely be more whistle-blowers. Failure to report puts the individual, project, and the organization at risk.

Project managers are responsible for ensuring that all ethical dilemmas are dealt with, the more serious ones being reported to the appropriate people or entities. They also must work to guarantee that all the efforts of the project comply with laws, regulations, processes, and procedures related to unethical situations and transgressions.

5.9.3 Performance and Ethics

These ethical dilemmas are strongly interrelated with dealing with sensitive people issues (Table 5.8) that can turn into major problems if not addressed right away.

5.9.3.1 Revealing Privileged Information

Information, as mentioned earlier, is vital to the success of an organization. It should be treated as a valuable asset and should receive the same treatment as a project involving a partnership with another company if there is one. In other words, it should be treated like gold. Some people

TABLE 5.8

Performance and Ethics

	Compliance	Effectiveness	Accurate and Timely Information	Efficiency	Protection of Resources
Revealing privileged information	√				√
Not confronting problems up front		√		√	

unfortunately talk too much, especially in a public forum, revealing information that even key stakeholders do not know anything about. Such reckless behavior can result in a loss of valuable information to competitors and may lead to litigation by parties injured by the revelation.

Everyone on the team should follow the policies and procedures related to privileged information. In some cases, compliance with any laws and regulations should be guaranteed. It also may be necessary to identify and protect information that is deemed critical to the project as well as prevent open discussions on certain topics in the presence of people who do not need to know.

5.9.3.2 Not Confronting Problems Up Front

Not all problems are ethical in nature, but the failure to address a serious problem is an ethical dilemma. Allowing a serious problem to exist under the radar while knowing it exists is representative of a lack of due diligence as well as a failure in exercising professional responsibilities as a project manager. Some project managers and other stakeholders, however, like to pretend something never happened and believe that addressing it in some way is an admission of an ethical failure.

Confronting problems up front can be encouraged in several ways. An atmosphere of trust can be engendered by encouraging open discussion and sharing of information. Issues can be brought up at team meetings and other sessions to maintain awareness of problems and even to come up with solutions. Metrics can be implemented and one-on-one or group sessions held regularly to identify and solve problems.

5.9.4 Perception and Ethics

These ethical dilemmas may have the appearance of being unethical. In actuality, they may not be issues at all but require further investigation to determine if there is some substance behind them (Table 5.9).

5.9.4.1 Deception

This one is essentially faking it. It is tied closely with massaging feedback and lying. Often, the lines among these three and others are blurred. Deception is giving the impression of one thing while doing another. The intent, in other words, is to lead people astray. Some people can do this very

TABLE 5.9

Perception and Ethics

	Compliance	Effectiveness	Accurate and Timely Information	Efficiency	Protection of Resources
Deception	√		√		
Not emphasizing the overall interests of a project		√		√	
Deliberately attempting to damage company reputation and product image	√				√

skillfully almost to the point of being a master propagandist; they tell only one side of a story but portray it all in such a way that others think they are getting the whole story. Unfortunately, such behavior can lead to people seeking legal action because they were misled. It also kills credibility.

Several actions can be taken to minimize the occurrence and impact of deception. All data and information about a project can be reviewed separately by two or more people. Metrics can be put in place and data scrubbed prior to calculating them. At meetings, people can be encouraged to act as a devil's advocate to challenge insights, comments, and ideas that seem to prevail.

5.9.4.2 Not Emphasizing the Overall Interests of a Project

All projects serve a purpose; all efforts should be directed toward satisfying the reason for its existence. If other people gain from its success, then all the better. However, sometimes people—including the project manager—think that the project exists solely to serve their needs and at the expense of the project itself. When the needs of the project are overridden by the needs of individuals, then collaboration becomes difficult if not impossible. Project performance begins to suffer as people jockey for advantage, and the entire project becomes politicized. Rework and missed goals and objectives are just some of the results when stakeholders do not emphasize the overall interests of a project.

Certain actions can be taken to discourage and perhaps prevent deemphasizing the overall interests of a project. When an issue or problem arises, team members can be encouraged to look at the big picture first. The purpose, goals, and objectives of the project can be reviewed at the beginning of all meetings. When issues and problems do arise, the impact of the purpose, goals, and objectives on the project can be described.

5.9.4.3 Deliberately Attempting to Damage Company Reputation and Product Image

Some people just have it out for the organization or project that they support. They may not have wanted to participate in it but have no other choice. They may not like the people or the management they work with. They may have been passed over for a promotion or a pay raise. Whatever the reason, they will do what they can to seek redress or payback. Not surprisingly, they may create or foment ethical dilemmas just to have the sweet taste of vengeance or revenge.

Not much can be done to prevent a deliberate attempt to damage company reputation and product image. About the best project managers can do is be aware of stakeholders who might take action and be careful what data, information, and other resources are entrusted to them.

5.10 FINAL THOUGHTS

In this chapter, a large number of ethical dilemmas were presented. Many of these are interrelated, meaning that they overlap in their purpose and effects. Some of them do not appear as ethical dilemmas but have serious ethical impacts. Others are so blatant as ethical dilemmas that it boggles the imagination that they exist, yet they occur more often than people like to think. Many of them happen, too, not by design but by accident. Whether by design or accident, they have to be addressed, of course. But project managers also need to uncover the intent. If an ethical situation or transgression arises because one or more people intended it to happen, then the response must take on a higher degree of intensity.

5.11 GETTING STARTED CHECKLIST

Question		Yes	No
1.	Have you considered the following contextual circumstances of your project contributing to the likelihood of an ethical issue arising?		
	Temporary nature of the project		
	Finiteness of the project		
	The pressure of time		
	Temporary relationships		
2.	Have you considered the potential ethical issues arising during each of the five major processes of project management?		
	Initiating		
	Planning		
	Executing		
	Monitoring and controlling		
	Closing		
3.	Do you consider ethical issues from the following categories of ethical topics?		
	Compliance		
	Effectiveness		
	Accurate and timely information		
	Efficiency		
	Protection of resources		
4.	Do you look out for the following potential ethical issues during the initiating process of your project?		
	Low-balling		
	Omitting key stakeholders		
	Misalignment with organizational goals		
	Conflict of interest		
	Not clarifying expectations		

Continued

Question		Yes	No
	Lying to win contract		
	Sabotaging relationship with certain stakeholders		
	Not engaging in good faith negotiations		
5.	Do you look out for the following potential ethical issues during the planning process of your project?		
	Padding		
	No accountability		
	Lying		
6.	Do you look out for the following potential ethical issues during the executing process of your project?		
	Mischarging		
	Misinformation or disinformation		
	Straying from plan without authorization		
	Violating confidentiality		
	Jeopardizing working relationships		
	Violating employee rights		
	Vilifying peers		
	Deliberately underperforming		
	Squashing dissent		
	Ignoring needs of team members		
	Lacking reliable, consistent treatment of team members		
	Not encouraging collaboration		
	Dismissing without cause		
	Sending a defective product to the customer		
	Unauthorized copying		
	Lacking consistent enforcement of standards		
7.	Do you look out for the following potential ethical issues during the monitoring and controlling process of your project?		
	Misreporting		
	Massaging or not sharing information with critical stakeholders		
	Not using reliable data to generate information		

Question		Yes	No
	Not using plans to report progress		
	Deliberately not reporting bad news		
	Inflating expense reports		
	Destroying or stealing vital information		
8.	Do you look out for the following potential ethical issues during the closing process of your project?		
	Not delivering results as promised		
	Not satisfying contractual requirements		
	Falsifying records		
9.	Have you considered the following ethical issues that apply to two or more of the five project management processes as they relate to people?		
	Allowing toxic culture to exist		
	Incivility		
	Harassment		
	Violation of privacy		
	Retaliation		
	Coercion		
	Not respecting values		
	Not providing honest feedback		
	Treating people inequitably		
	Lacking personal responsibility		
	Spreading malicious rumors		
	Misusing power and position		
	Discriminating		
	Encouraging or not dealing with infighting		
	Not treating everyone fairly and respectfully		
	Not stopping hidden agendas		
	Exploiting people		
	Deliberately maliciously damaging reputations		

Continued

	Question	Yes	No
10.	Have you considered the following ethical issues that apply to two or more of the five project management processes as they relate to process?		
	Receiving inappropriate entertainment and gifts		
	Conflict of interest relationship with customers and suppliers		
	Lacking due diligence and due care		
	Lacking objectivity and independence		
	Massaging feedback		
	Unequal access to information and other key resources		
	Engaging in illicit activities		
	Not reporting unethical behavior		
11.	Have you considered the following ethical issues that apply to two or more of the five project management processes as they relate to performance?		
	Revealing privileged information		
	Not confronting problems upfront		
12.	Have you considered the following ethical issues that apply to two or more of the five project management processes as they relate to perception?		
	Deception		
	Not emphasizing the overall interests of a project		
	Deliberately attempting to damage company reputation and product image		

6

Ethics and Project Governance

In the ideal world, everyone is ethical. There is no need for oversights, signatures of approval, cross-checking, or separating duties because everyone does the "right thing." Unfortunately, that ideal does not exist; Shangri-La remains a dream. That, of course, does not mean that people as a general rule are unethical; it indicates that once in awhile persons with unethical intentions can join the team, creating an environment that demands effective governance disciplines for a project.

6.1 WHAT IS GOVERNANCE?

The idea of governance on a project is a relatively new concept often associated with much larger organizations. Few people think of it as part of project management, but it is very important, for without it a project becomes nothing more than an unfocused group that achieves very little over time and consumes more resources than are necessary.

Governance is identifying and implementing the policies, processes, procedures, tools, and techniques for achieving specific goals and objectives. These policies and procedures are often associated with efficiency and effectiveness, in terms of achieving goals and objectives with the least amount of waste or at minimal cost. Some of the more well-known goals and objectives are maximizing benefits and minimizing costs, providing business value, setting and meeting customer expectations, adding structure to ensure better predictability of performance, ensuring improved quality of output, meeting expectations, resolving conflict, and balancing short- and long-term perspectives when considering the relationship of cost, schedule, quality, scope, and risk. Rarely, if ever, is there any emphasis on ensuring ethical performance of the stakeholders or at least laying the groundwork for increasing the likelihood of ethical behavior. Every effort should be made to minimize the probability of unethical activities.

It is safe to say, therefore, that good governance on a project consists of applying good project management disciplines that enable successful completion of a project, depending on what the criteria for success is. Ethics plays an important role in the effective application of these disciplines. The reason is simple: Unethical decisions and actions affect the quality of the output of those disciplines, much like bad data generate unreliable information. Therefore, ethics cannot be divorced from project management.

Take the following example. A customer wants a new information system developed. To win the contract, the vendor commits to an unrealistic schedule and budget with the anticipation that this will lead to more work in the future through work orders and enhancements. Both parties sign a contract and then a charter with the vendor knowing all too well that the parameters for the project are unrealistic. The plans, all predicated on an unrealistic contract, charter, and scope of work, will eventually lead to failure. The customer, out of ignorance, agrees to a series of work orders that overrun the budget and slips major milestones. Reporting throughout the project contains unreliable data that generate poor information, leading to bad decisions. In the end, the customer ends up paying for a system that does not meet expectations, principally because of the unethical behavior of the vendor.

Instituting governance on projects is not easy. One reason is that governance is construed as instituting control, and to some extent that is true. However, governance also provides structure so that more is done with a minimal amount of waste. Still, some people fear governance thinking it might constrain them. Another reason is that people disagree as to how much governance is necessary on a project. Often, the amount of governance depends on the culture of the overall organization and what it views as sufficient breadth and depth being implemented. Still another reason, and tied to the last point, is that governance means something different for each stakeholder. Some will view it as following a rigid methodology, whereas others see it as simply providing a guideline on what to do.

6.2 WHAT ARE CONTROLS?

Basically, controls help to address five concerns:

1. *Compliance* involves adherence to policies, procedures, laws, and regulations.
2. *Effectiveness* involves ensuring the achievement of goals and objectives.
3. *Accurate and timely information* involves ensuring that the right people get the right information of the right amount in the right format at the right time
4. *Efficiency* involves ensuring that resources are used in a manner that reduces waste.
5. *Protection of resources* involves ensuring physical and logical safekeeping of the project's resources.

A control is a measure put in place to protect the project from threats, such as an ethical issue or transgression. A failure in the effectiveness of a control is one where it does not effectively protect a project, in this case from an ethical issue or violation. Project managers can employ three types of controls to ensure all five categories increase the likelihood of ethical behavior on a project: (1) preventive; (2) detective; and (3) corrective. Preventive controls take effect before a threat, such as an ethical issue or transgression, occurs. Often they entail putting strategies in place to deal with offsets or to deter their occurrence. Detective controls reveal a threat, such as an ethical issue or transgression, has occurred and report it to the appropriate people. Corrective controls require taking action to rectify the situation and ensure that circumstances get back to normal. Controls can fit one or more categories, depending on their application; they are not necessarily mutually exclusive.

Table 6.1 contains a list of common controls that could be used to address a wide range of ethical threats, issues, and transgressions.

6.3 WHAT IS RISK?

A risk represents a potential vulnerability to a system, whether automated or manual. A threat is a risk that is applicable to a project based on

TABLE 6.1

Sample of Common Controls

Common Control	Type of Control	Reason	Examples
Perform testing	Preventive, Detective	Ensure compliance with standards to ensure that no defective product is released to the customer	Look for deviations from standards
Develop reports	Detective	Monitor and control performance to ensure people receive a "true" picture of what is occurring on a project	Generate ad hoc and regular reports to performance according to plan
Perform statistical analysis	Detective	Detect variances that rely on facts and data rather than conjecture	Discover excessive cost, schedule, and scope thresholds
Apply change control	Preventive, Corrective	Achieve goals and objectives to ensure that the customer knows what to expect when the project is complete	Review and approve or disapprove changes to cost, schedule, and cope baselines
Conduct reviews and approvals	Preventive	Ensure that the project meets expectations of the customer and other stakeholders and that nothing escapes under the radar	Review reports for accuracy prior to release
Log activities	Detective	Establish an audit trail so reviewers can understand the origin of contents in reports	Keep track of issues and follow up on whether addressed
Prepare documentation	Preventive, Detective	Keep a historical record of decisions and actions to demonstrate either compliance or lack thereof to policies, procedures, charter, and contract	Draft memorandums, lessons learned
Implement access control	Preventive, Detective	Restrict tools, data, and supplies from general access to ensure the resources of the project and the entire company protected	Restrict access to proprietary information to individuals or organizations having a need to know

TABLE 6.1 (continued)

Sample of Common Controls

Common Control	Type of Control	Reason	Examples
Ensure segregation of duties	Preventive	Restrict a person from having complete control over a task or information so that individual does not compromise the organization	Have one person develop the deliverable and another review it
Adopt best practices	Preventive	Apply processes, tools, and techniques that enhance project performance	Use practice standards, frameworks, or methodologies advocated by professional organizations that stakeholders know will produce expected results
Institute metrics	Preventive, detective	Provide visibility of how well the project is progressing	Use earned value management
Assign accountability for results	Preventive	Encourage people to assume responsibility for results	Identify roles, accountabilities, and authorities

probability and impact. Controls can be put in place to reduce the impact of a threat. In some cases, threats can be prevented or mitigated should they occur; in other cases, a decision may be made to accept the event (a realized threat) because the impact is inconsequential. Projects can face a wide range of ethical dilemmas, and the project manager needs to be able to apply an appropriate strategy to deal with them should the threats become realized.

An important distinction between a risk and an issue needs to be made at this point. A risk is something that could occur in the future; for example, an unethical risk may be when a stakeholder might release proprietary information to the public. An issue is something that exists now and is consequently no longer a risk; for example, an unethical issue is a stakeholder who has already released proprietary information to the public. Ideally, as many risks as possible should be identified and strategies put in place to deal with them if they should arise, or action should be taken in advance to deal with them should they become an issue.

6.4 EFFECTIVE RISK MANAGEMENT

Although risks, threats, or issues on projects cannot be eliminated, the likelihood of their occurrence and impact can be reduced by taking several actions.

One, exercise due diligence and due care regarding ethical issues and transgressions. Due diligence is putting the necessary measures in place to decrease the likelihood of a risk occurring and, if it does, minimize its impact. Due care is actually implementing what was identified and developed under due diligence. It makes little sense to identify and develop policies, processes, procedures, tools, and techniques if they are not going to be actually implemented.

Two, if an ethical risk, threat, or issue does arise, determine whether the controls in place have managed to eliminate or mitigate the impact. If an ethical threat has occurred, it is necessary to know if the controls worked to prevent it from having a negative effect on the project and the organization and also so that a project of a similar nature has an idea of the effectiveness of the control.

Three, if an ethical issue or transgression does arise, determine the intent behind its occurrence. Many ethical issues and transgressions arise out of ignorance rather than intent. The degree of intention and their corresponding impacts will determine the breadth and depth of control being exercised.

Four, perform a risk assessment for the project. This should include looking at the ethical risks to the project. These risks are often overlooked and are partly why some projects and companies find themselves dealing with them in a reactive rather proactive mode. The risk assessment enables the likelihood or probability and impact of a risk to be determined and the appropriate preventive, detective, or corrective controls to be in place to deal with it.

Five, look at the context of the project. The context can tell quite a bit about the ethical threats facing the project, the likelihood, and the impact. Some of the contextual factors to consider include the tone at the top of an organization, market conditions, financial state of the economy, previous history of an organization dealing with ethical issues and transgressions, relationship among key stakeholders, and the amount of time and other resources needed to complete a project.

Six, revisit the risk assessment from time to time. The context of a project changes over time, and what seemed significant from an ethical standpoint at one time may no longer be so. Stakeholders change, the scope changes, and other factors like the economy can all change, sometimes overnight. That's why you should revisit the risk assessment on a regular basis or when something changes.

Seven, when revisiting a risk assessment, be sure also to look at the effectiveness of existing controls vis-à-vis risks. It may become apparent that certain controls are no longer useful and therefore need to be replaced. Or additional controls may need to be instituted to strengthen the existing ones. In addition, if a control was implemented to address a risk it may have created another risk requiring additional risk management.

Eight, maintain objectivity and independence when conducting a risk assessment as it relates to ethical issues and transgressions. Allowing room for prejudices leads to out-of-control circumstances. The danger is looking for confirmation of decisions and actions, which can lead to cloudy judgment. Bias and overconfidence can be a killer in decision making.

Nine, consider establishing some type of heuristic, or rule of thumb, for determining materiality for a control weakness, such as an ethical issue or transgression. Determining materiality is relatively easy when something is quantifiable, such as exceeding a cost threshold of 10 percent. The challenge is when something occurs that is more qualitative in nature, such as a large number of complaints from team members. Yet materiality enables a determination to be made of how significant a threat is if and when it occurs and the extent of the response to address it. That's where judgment becomes important as well as the data and information that go into it. If there is any doubt as to what extent the response should be to a risk, consider both the likelihood and the impact and then exercise the prudent man rule, which basically states what a reasonable person would do in a specific situation.

Ten, recognize that no matter how well a risk assessment is performed that ethical risks or any other type of risk can never be eliminated from a project. Project managers can deal only with what they know might happen, and that depends on a limited amount of information. In addition, the information that is known is constantly changing in quality and quantity. Ethical issues and transgressions will arise no matter how many attempts are made to identify and prepare for them.

Finally, when the risk assessment is performed from an ethical perspective, identify the following for each ethical issue:

- Description
- Likelihood or probability of occurrence
- Impact
- Potential preventive, detective, and corrective controls
- Risk ownership

Of course, the risk assessment should be reviewed with key stakeholders on a periodic basis. The context of the project will likely change; consequently, the risks will too as well as the attributes of the existing ones.

6.5 FINAL THOUGHTS

Governance on projects demonstrates due diligence and due care, two important actions for minimizing the chance of an ethical situation or transgression occurring. Risk management is a key tool for demonstrating both. While risk management cannot eliminate all risks, it does help preclude the occurrence of known threats and, if they do occur, enables project managers to deal with them in a way that eradicates or minimizes their impact.

6.6 GETTING STARTED CHECKLIST

	Question	Yes	No
1.	Do you have effective governance on your project?		
	If not, what can you do to improve governance on your project?		
2.	Do you have effective controls in place to give reasonable assurance of the following?		
	That policies, procedures, laws, and regulations (compliance) are adhered to		
	That goals and objectives (effectiveness) are achieved		
	That the right people get the right amount of information in the right format at the right time (accurate and timely information)		
	That the resources are used in a manner that reduces waste (efficiency)		

Question		Yes	No
	Physical and logical safekeeping of the project's resources (protection of resources)		
2.	For each ethical threat or issue, do you have any of one or more of the following controls in place?		
	Preventive		
	Detective		
	Corrective		
3.	Have you identified threats that will require any of the following controls?		
	Perform testing		
	Develop reports		
	Perform statistical analysis		
	Apply change control		
	Conduct reviews and approvals		
	Log activities		
	Prepare documentation		
	Implement access control		
	Ensure segregation of duties		
	Adopt best practices		
	Institute metrics		
	Assign accountability for results		
4.	Do you need to have controls in place for the following ethical threats or issues?		
	Misreporting (underreporting or overreporting)		
	Deliberately withholding bad news		
	Inflating expense reports		
	Destroying or stealing vital information		
	Massaging or not sharing information with critical stakeholders		
	Not using reliable data to generate information		
	Ignoring needs of team members		
	Lacking reliable, consistent treatment of team members		

Continued

Question	Yes	No
Not encouraging collaboration		
Dismissing without cause		
Sending a defective product to customer		
Unauthorized copying		
Lacking consistent enforcement of standards		
Straying from plan without authorization		
Violating confidentiality		
Jeopardizing working relationships		
Vilifying peers		
Violating employee rights		
Deliberately underperforming		
Squashing dissent		
Using unknowingly false information		
Providing unreliable cost and schedule baselines		
Not having a work breakdown structure		
Understanding work effort		
Mischarging		
Misinformation or disinformation		
Sabotaging relationship with vendors		
Not engaging in good faith negotiations		
Padding		
Not having accountability		
Lying		
Allowing groupthink		
Low-balling		
Omitting key stakeholders		
Misaligning with organizational goals		
Conflicts of interest		
Not clarifying expectations		
Lying to win contract		
Not using plans to report progress		

Question	Yes	No
Not delivering results as promised		
Not satisfying contractual requirements		
Falsifying records		
Allowing a toxic culture to exist		
Incivility		
Harassment		
Violation of privacy		
Retaliation		
Coercion		
Not respecting values		
Not providing honest feedback		
Treating people inequitably		
Lacking personal responsibility		
Spreading malicious rumors		
Misusing power or position		
Encouraging or not dealing with infighting		
Not treating everyone fairly or respectfully		
Not stopping hidden agendas		
Exploiting people		
Deliberately maliciously damaging reputation		
Receiving inappropriate gifts and entertainment		
Conflict of interest relationship with customers and suppliers		
Lacking due diligence and due care		
Lacking objectivity and independence		
Massaging feedback		
Unequal access to information and other key resources		
Engaging in illicit activities		
Not reporting unethical behavior		
Revealing privileged information		
Not confronting problems upfront		

Continued

Question		Yes	No
	Not emphasizing the overall interests of the project		
	Deliberately attempting to damage company reputation and product image		
5.	Have you done the following to reduce or eliminate ethical threats or address issues to your project?		
	Exercise due diligence and due care		
	Determine whether the controls in place have managed to eliminate or mitigate the impact		
	If an unethical threat or issue does occur, determine the intent behind its occurrence		
	Perform a risk assessment for your project		
	Look at the context of your project		
	Revisit the risks from time to time		
	Look at the effectiveness of existing controls vis-à-vis risks or issues		
	Maintain your objectivity and independence when conducting a risk assessment		
	Consider establishing some type of heuristic, or rule of thumb, for determining materiality of a control weakness		
	Recognize that no matter how well you do a risk assessment, you can never, ever eliminate ethical risks or issues		
6.	When doing a risk assessment, did you identify the following items?		
	Description		
	Likelihood or probability of occurrence		
	Impact		
	Preventive, detective, or corrective controls		
	Risk ownership		

7

Ethics and the Law

Ethics is often erroneously confused with compliance with the law. In reality, ethics is much broader than the law. In this chapter, however, the focus is on compliance with the law.

Ethics and law seem tightly intertwined for obvious reasons. Violation of laws related to ethics can lead to fines and penalties for organizations and individuals, can end in debarment, or can cause a public relations disaster. Ethical situations and transgressions that do not involve the law, more often than not, are dealt with in a much quieter way. The legal penalties for violations are often substantial and, consequently, demand, immediate attention.

7.1 THE RELATIONSHIP BETWEEN LAW AND ETHICS

It behooves organizations, and in some instances individuals, to keep the following guidelines in mind when considering ethics and the law.

First, recognize that compliance includes more than the law—for example, adhering to policies, procedures, and methodologies of an organization. Most organizations circle around compliance with the law, but not always. For example, compliance with a methodology may not involve compliance with the law but may require compliance with management direction or a specific contract with a customer.

Second, recognize that compliance is not passive; it is very active. Organizations, at all levels, must make a concerted effort to demonstrate compliance with the law. The absence of an ethical situation or transgression does not mean compliance with the law. More often than not, compliance with the law must be demonstrated, meaning exercising such concepts as due diligence and due care. For example, tests should be administered to ensure compliance with quality standards dictated by the law; it cannot be assumed that compliance will just happen.

Third, understand that noncompliance requires taking corrective action. Failure to comply, especially if awareness of its existence occurs and nothing is done, can result in stiff penalties both for the organization and the individuals involved. For example, it is dangerous to assume that a serious violation of a law on the project will go away simply by ignoring it or hoping that no one says anything to be absolved of responsibility.

Fourth, have a good understanding of any applicable laws, but do not act as an attorney. Project managers manage projects; that is their expertise. Unless they have a strong legal background or are an attorney, they should rely on experts to help with questions regarding the law. Oftentimes, the law can be vague and convoluted, and interpreting without the expertise can have dire consequences for the organization and involved individuals. For example, export laws can be very complex and the company's attorney can help interpret them.

Fifth, realize that compliance does not stop unethical behavior; it simply minimizes the probability of occurrence. Just because a law exists and an organization embraces the law does not mean people on the team or the parent organization are obeying it. Compliance requires ongoing awareness and, in some cases, continuous monitoring. For example, it makes good sense to have an idea of what laws apply to the project and to revisit them during the course of the project to determine the degree of compliance.

Sixth, recognize that noncompliance can result from internal and external circumstances. For example, partnerships and other strategic alliances in which the project may be involved do not necessarily exempt individuals or the project from responsibility for compliance; a close working relationship could lead to legal complications without anyone realizing it.

Seventh, be aware of the ethical laws applicable to the project and have a good understanding of the content and scope of those laws. When it comes to compliance, knowledge is the best protection. Again, when in doubt, contact the experts. For example, large companies especially have procurement specialists, lawyers, and contract specialists available for consultation.

Eighth, do not let current conduct and custom be a substitute for compliance with the law. Conduct and custom are good guides, but both may be tolerating noncompliance. For example, what may be customary in China or Italy may not be legal according to the home country's laws.

Ninth, don't gamble with obeying the law by calculating the acceptable loss or threshold in terms of fines, because fines are only one part of the equation. There is also the potential for debarment, imprisonment, and a tarnished reputation, which are incalculable and can go way beyond the purview and time frame of the project.

Tenth, corporate social responsibility dictates that individuals and the project comply with the law. Some companies have considerable economic, social, and political power that can impact society in many ways. Failure to comply with relevant laws can result in negative consequences that go beyond the law. The same applies to a large project or program. Knowingly, and sometimes unknowingly, violating the law can harm people, their trust, and the organization's credibility as an institution. For example, a blatant violation of hazmat laws not only has legal ramifications but also can cause physical and emotional problems.

It is a fact of life in business that the laws originate from many different jurisdictions. In the United States, businesses must follow federal law originating not just from congress but also from many branches and agencies in the United States. Some of these agencies are semiprivate, while others are public. Here is a sample list of agencies and other entities at the federal level that you or your organization may have to deal with and comply with their regulations:

- Bureau of Alcohol, Tobacco, Firearms, and Explosives
- Bureau of Industry and Security
- Commodity Credit Corporation
- Council on Environmental Quality
- Customs and Border Protection
- Department of Commerce
- Department of Treasury
- Directorate of Defense Trade Controls
- Equal Employment Opportunity Commission
- Federal Financial Institutions Examination Council
- Food and Drug Administration
- International Trade Administration
- National Labor Relations Board
- Occupational Health and Safety Administration
- Office of Federal Procurement Policy
- Office of Government Standards
- Overseas Private Investment Corporation

- Securities and Exchange Commission
- U.S. Customs Service
- U.S. Export-Import Bank
- U.S. Federal Trade Commission
- U.S. Trade Representative

In addition to the federal institutions, a wide of array of laws exist at the state and local levels as well as in other countries and within specific juris-dictions for each one. As if that is not enough, businesses may have to follow international guidelines and rules, some of which may be public or private:

- Asia-Pacific Economic Cooperation (APEC)
- Caux Round Table Business Principles of Ethics
- Council of Europe Cybercrime Convention
- European Union (EU)
- General Agreement on Tariffs and Trade (GATT)
- International Monetary Fund (IMF)
- North American Free Trade Agreement (NAFTA)
- Organization of Petroleum Exporting Countries (OPEC)
- United Nations Conference on Trade and Development (UNCTAD)
- United Nations Convention on Contracts for International Sale of Goods (CISG)
- World Trade Organization (WTO)

The bottom line is that it is necessary to know, based on the scope of the project, at least what laws apply to the project and then to become familiar with them. If there are questions or doubts, check with the appropriate legal experts.

7.2 KEY LEGAL TERMS

While it may not be necessary to know all the laws, it is prudent to be familiar with some basic legal terms and principles as discussed from the perspective of American jurisprudence. What follows is a brief description of some of the key legal terms that are often used on a project. These terms were selected for project management relevancy and are not meant to be exhaustive.

Acceptance: An agreement to accept the product or service being delivered

Agent: A person or organization acting on behalf of a customer or client

Arbitration: A binding decision by a third party

Bond: A promise to pay if there is a failure to perform

Breach: A failure to perform according to contract, either in whole or part

Condition: A requirement specified in a contract

Conflict of interest: A relationship that compromises the objectivity, independence, and loyalty to a business entity

Consideration: Also referred to as payment or tender; an exchange is either monetary or nonmonetary, such as an offset agreement (e.g., exchanging products for services) for the development and delivery of a product or service

Contract: A legal agreement that binds two or more parties to create a product or deliver a service

Copyright: An exclusive right to use original work; others require permission from the original author to use

Damages: Physical and nonphysical injuries a person or organization experiences as a result of a failure to perform

Defendant: A person or organization charged with committing a violation of law per plaintiff

Delegation of duties: The transfer of obligations to another party without abdicating responsibility for results

Delivery: The product or service within the control of the customer

Due process: Laws protecting the rights of individuals vis-à-vis the government

Duty: An obligation to perform

Equity: The application of principles to compensate for the shortcomings or inequities of current laws and rules

Exoneration: An agreement not to hold a party liable for loss or failure to perform

Felony: A criminal act that results in incarceration for one or more years or is legislated as such

Forbearance: Prevented from performing an act, such as a service

Fraud: A deliberate act to deceive by altering facts or making deliberate misstatements

Good faith: Knowledge or awareness of any defect in the product or service delivered to the customer

Liability: A civil wrong

Mediation: Nonbinding settlement of a dispute through a third party

Misdemeanor: A violation of law that results in incarceration for less than 1 year or is not designated a felony

Misrepresentation: A statement of fact falsely made without deception

Negligence: Not exercising appropriate action, resulting in harm to a person or organization

Offer: A person or organization expressing intent to enter into an agreement

Patent: Exclusive rights to an invention

Plaintiff: The individual or organization filing a lawsuit against a defendant

Precedent: A court decision setting the standard for future legal decisions

Principal: A person or organization that hires an agent to act on its behalf

Privity: A chain of relationships that must be followed

Prosecutor: Begins criminal proceedings against a defendant

Remedy: Activities to enforce payment of damages due to a legal injury

Repudiation: Refusal to perform one or more clauses of a contract

Rescission: One party decides to no longer follow a contract due to another party failing to execute according to the specified terms and conditions

Right: The capacity of a person or organization to require performance of an action by another party

Trademark: A symbol identifying a product or service

Waiver: A release of an obligation or duty

Warranty: A promise made in respect to the performance of a product

7.3 KEY LEGAL PRINCIPLES AND CONCEPTS

It is important to understand these categories of laws since they may affect the management of projects:

Administrative law: Laws passed for managing the affairs of government agencies

Civil law: A body of law established by nation states regarding the rights of its citizens

Common law: Legal rules setting precedents based on custom and their application by courts to make decisions

Criminal law: Body of law dealing with crimes and punishment

Procedural law: Rules followed by a court governing its activities
Statutory law: Laws passed by legislative bodies
Substantive law: Laws defining rights and responsibilities of individuals

Here are some legal principles and concepts to keep in mind as they relate to ethics and the law from the perspective of project management. These can help you avoid trouble.

First, recognize that all projects have a time of performance, meaning that projects start and finish within an agreed on time frame. This time of performance is often reflected in a contract and a charter, and in some cases, particularly with external customers, penalty payments are imposed for late delivery. All project plans should be predicated on meeting this timeline. A good practice, of course, is to look at all the options to determine the best approach to meet the timeline.

Second, understand that they involve some indication of an adequacy of performance, meaning that the project management and products or services must meet certain minimum standards. Failure to meet those minimum standards will impact the quality of output, possibly resulting in a legal violation, with the contract or governmental standards. Project managers should work closely with their legal, procurement, and quality organizations to help them ascertain ways to ensure compliance with adequacy of performance on their projects.

Third, establish and maintain an audit trail of the work performed, which serves as evidence of due diligence and due care, both important in case litigation arises. It also enables taking the appropriate corrective action if there is a violation of law. Some stakeholders believe that an audit trail will simply put their projects and parent organization in a legal mess should noncompliance occur. In reality, a lack of an audit trail raises red flags as an indicator that a failure to comply with a contract or a certain law occurred and, therefore, may warrant further investigation. On some projects, especially those related to the Sarbanes-Oxley Act and the federal government, a mere lack of an audit trail is a noncompliant action with the law.

Fourth, be aware of potential areas of fraud. While you don't need to go looking for them, keep in mind some of the indicators of fraud, such as people under personal financial pressure or experiencing stress or other personal problems (e.g., drugs), excessive travel, and entertainment expenses of individuals seeking reimbursement by the project or company. These are known as red flags. Fraud has become a topic of interest lately because of the magnitude of its occurrence. Because of it, companies and their leadership have been destroyed. The misperception is that fraud matters and occurs only with senior stakeholders; the reality is that it occurs at all levels.

Fifth, control access to critical or privileged information. This control should cover proprietary, secrets, and personal identifiable information. Information should be provided on a need-to-know basis; failure to protect critical or privileged information can have a host of consequences to the project manager, to other people, and especially to others impacted by the release. This control has become much more difficult in today's environment with the rise of thumb drives, CD/DVD burners, and logs, making difficult the job of controlling access. It is imperative, therefore, that project managers make every effort to comply with the law if for no other reason than to protect themselves and their organization should an unauthorized release of data and information occur.

Sixth, apply project management disciplines and techniques to the project as a demonstration of due diligence and due care. In some areas, project management disciplines are viewed as being bureaucratic. For internal projects, that attitude may be permissible, but for commercial contracts, especially those of a high financial amount that could sink a company by failing, such an approach is wrought with danger. In this case, angry shareholders will likely want to recover their losses and seek vengeance in other ways (e.g., termination of key stakeholders).

Seventh, provide oversight of suppliers and contractors related to the project. They are members of the team. While all the legal protections may be in place, the reality is that if some major compliance problem exists and it is committed by the suppliers or contractors, the likelihood is good that the buyer (in your case) will be construed, whether in actuality or appearance, as being involved in the noncompliance incident. If your company is the one with the big name that everyone knows and the vendor or contractor is not, the firm's reputation will be tarnished.

Eighth, be aware of the dangers associated with receiving gifts and other favors from vendors. Simple gifts of what may seem of minimal value can give the appearance of a conflict of interest. These gifts need to be approved in advance, especially if they involve a certain threshold value. Going out to dinner or on a joint golf outing can be construed as a conflict of interest, at least during the course of the project. The fundamental question, of course, is who pays for what?

Ninth, conduct a good risk assessment. This action will enable identifying the key risks that could impact a project. One of the major results is identifying risks, some of which may be legal ones that have a high impact to a project. Knowing what those risks are will enable the project manager to determine the appropriate level of disciplines to ensure compliance. A risk assessment will enable determining the material impact of a breach with a specific law.

Tenth, know the contract for the project. While it is not necessary to be a lawyer or a contract administrator, it is a good practice to know the terms and conditions of the contract. This knowledge ensures that team member actions do not violate the terms and conditions. A simple decision that may at first make reasonable sense to move a project forward can possibly mean that certain terms and conditions had been violated. For example, the project manager or team members violate the principle of privity and bypass the prime contractor and manage the subcontractor directly.

Eleventh, understand that few, if any, projects operate in a legal "bubble," meaning that the tentacles of the law stretch far into most organizations today. For example, many laws that deal with the relationships among employees (e.g., harassment, workplace safety, labor contracts) can easily be violated without ever realizing it. Having a good knowledge of such laws can help preclude noncompliance from becoming a major legal issue. At least when something does occur, appropriate action can be taken to become compliant with the law.

Twelfth, apply the proper exercise of authority. Too many times, especially project managers without much practical experience and knowledge, think that as a project manager they have complete control to make decisions and act in a way that borders on authoritarianism. Such behavior not only reflects a lack of maturity but can also put a project in dangerous legal problems. For example, project managers may make a decision to commit an organization to procurement contract when they may not have the authority to do so.

Thirteenth, comply with all internal and external audits and investigations. While that makes common sense, it does not always happen, especially if certain stakeholders—including the project manager—lack the confidence that they are in compliance with the law regarding a certain issue. When requested to provide information, cooperation is essential; otherwise, it could raise red flags and be construed as lying or hiding facts and data regarding a noncompliance issue.

172 • Ethics and Project Management

Fourteenth, apply effective controls on a project, especially if they are related to compliance. Putting in good project management disciplines is a good start, but that may not be enough to ensure compliance with applicable laws. It may be necessary to determine additional controls. There are essentially three types of controls: (1) preventive controls, which are instituted to minimize the probability and impact of something going awry, such as implementing segregation of duties; (2) detective controls, which indicate that something has happened, such as a report indicating that a certain threshold is being reached could be construed as a potential legal violation; and (3) corrective controls, which involve actions that are taken to fix any identified variance to policy, procedure, or law (i.e., the goal is to get back in compliance).

Finally, don't become a "latrine lawyer." In other words, don't take the law in your own hands. Just because people are project managers does not mean that they know everything including all the laws. Too many stakeholders confuse familiarity with expertise in regards to legal interpretation. It is good practice to become familiar with laws, but when it comes to legal interpretation it is best to consult the organization's legal or contracts staff for guidance.

7.4 NUMEROUS LAWS AND REGULATIONS

Project managers may find that they have to comply with a wide range of U.S. laws, depending on the purpose and scope of their projects. Following is a description of some of the more common laws. It is not meant to be exhaustive. These laws and regulations also may or may not apply to every project.

The laws can be grouped into categories. While these categories overlap like Venn diagrams, there are essentially (1) general, (2) environmental, (3) financial, (4) labor, (5) procurement, (6) international trade, and (7) information technology and security.

General laws and regulations deal with the relations among governments and businesses either under normal or emergency circumstances. They span a wide range of topics from the environment to finance.

- Federal sentencing guidelines on sentencing policies and practices regarding convictions for committing a federal crime

- Hobbs Act prohibits actual or attempted extortion or robbery related to interstate and foreign commerce
- International Emergency Economic Powers Act grants authority granted to the U.S. president to deal with a national emergency or threat to the economy or national security
- Organized Crime Control Act is famous for its Title IX, known as the RICO (Racketeer Influenced and Corrupt Organizations), which seeks to remove organized crime and racketeering from organizations engaged in interstate commerce
- Uniform Commercial Code (UCC) is a set of guidelines and principles governing the proper execution of commercial transactions to preclude commission of crimes, such as fraud

Environmental laws and regulations deal with the protection of the environment as well as ensuring the health and well-being of the general population and wildlife.

- Clean Air Act protects and improves air quality
- Clean Water Act provides quality standards for surface waters
- Endangered Species Act provides for the conservation of ecosystems for threatened and endangered species
- National Environmental Policy Act requires federal agencies to integrate environmental impacts when making decisions
- Oil Pollution Act establishes provisions for preventing and responding to oil spills, to include contingency planning by the federal government and business
- Resource Conservation and Recovery Act regulates the generation, transport, treatment, storage, and disposal of hazardous waste
- Safe Drinking Water Act establishes standards for the quality of drinking water as well as ensures their implementation across different governmental entities
- Superfund Amendment and Reauthorization Act covers emergency preparedness and response to hazardous chemicals across different governmental entities
- Toxic Substances Control Act covers reporting, recordkeeping, testing, importing, and disposing of chemicals

Financial laws and regulations deal with the monetary and conduct of commercial relationships between government and business as well as between businesses themselves. In some cases, they include protection of shareholders and the general population from a commercial relationship perspective.

- Anti-kickback Act strengthens the prohibition of contractors or subcontractors from receiving rewards or favorable treatment
- Bank Secrecy Act requires financial institutions to help the federal government to detect and prevent money laundering
- Clayton Act prohibits price discrimination
- False Claims Act prohibits falsely presenting fraudulent claims for payment or approval to the U.S. government
- Gramm-Leach-Bliley Act, also known as the Financial Services Modernization Act, repeals portions of the Glass-Steagall Act by allowing banks to engage in a broader array of financial activities
- Money Laundering Control Act makes it a criminal act to engage in money laundering
- Robinson-Patman Act prohibits unequal business competition in regards to the pricing of commodities and purchases
- Sarbanes-Oxley Act establishes legal requirements to improve the accuracy and reliability of financial disclosures to shareholders
- Sherman Anti-Trust Act prohibits restraint of trade at the interstate level

Labor laws and regulations deal with the relationship between management and employees as well as the hiring and release of human resources and their remuneration.

- Age Discrimination in Employment Act prohibits employers to release from or refuse employment to a person based on age
- Americans with Disability Act prohibits discrimination against individuals with disabilities and requires enforcement of standards specified in the law
- Civil Rights Act forbids discrimination based on sex and race in hiring, promoting, and firing
- Employee Retirement Income Security Act regulates employee pension and welfare benefit plans in the business environment
- Equal Pay Act prohibits employers from discriminating based on sex when paying wages

- Fair labor Standards Act prohibits child labor, sets a minimum wage, and establishes overtime pay
- Family and Medical Leave Act allows for employees to take up to 12 weeks of unpaid leave while retaining health benefits
- Immigration and Nationality Act sets general eligibility requirements to become a U.S. citizen
- Immigration Reform and Control Act controls and prevents illegal immigration into the United States
- National Labor Relations Act protects the rights of employees and employers in respect to collective bargaining
- Uniform Services Employment and Re-employment Rights Act prohibits discrimination in employment of veterans due to military service

Procurement laws and regulations deal with the contractual relationship with governments and among businesses when procuring resources and services.

- Federal acquisition regulations provides standard policies and procedures related to procuring goods and services
- Federal Acquisition Reform Act mandates full and open competition to meet the federal government's procurement requirements
- Procurement Integrity Act regulates the conduct of government employees participating in procurements and contract administration
- Truth in Negotiations Act requires fair and reasonable pricing in a noncompetitive environment and requires remedies for "defective" pricing regarding government contracts

International trade laws and regulations deal with import and export relationships among governments as well as restricting or preventing sensitive information and products being imported from or exported to specified governments.

- Arms Export Control Act:regulates the export of defense articles and services through the Department of State
- Customs Modernization Act:regulates the commercial operations of the U.S. Customs Service by streamlining the movement of goods via automation

- Export Administration Act:establishes a control list of technologies that could provide military potential to other nations and is administered through the Department of Defense
- Export Administration Regulations:regulates the control of specific exports and restricts their flow to countries not supportive of U.S. interest and is administered through the Department of Commerce
- Export Control Acts:restricts the import and export of certain defense munitions and services to specific individuals and governments
- Export Trading Company Act:enables U.S. companies to collaborate to streamline export operations and reduce costs and compete in the international market
- Foreign Corrupt Practices Act:prohibits making payments, such as bribes, to foreign government officials to obtain business
- International Traffic in Arms Regulations:regulates the export of defense articles and services under the Arms Export Control Act
- Webb-Pomerene Act:provides an exemption of U.S. businesses engaged in export trade from antitrust provisions, unless it restrains competition

Information technology and security laws and regulations deal with the use of technology and the protection of information and ideas.

- Computer Fraud and Abuse Act prohibits the unauthorized access of information (e.g., related to defense or finances) and provides penalties for such actions
- Copyright Law establishes exclusive usage rights for the creator of an original work
- Federal Information Security Management Act requires federal agencies to deploy security of information and technology supporting their operations whether through the government itself or contractors
- Patent Law allows exclusive right of inventors to use inventions exclusively for a period of time
- Privacy Act establishes a code of information practices governing the collection, management, and distribution of sensitive information about individuals
- Health Insurance Portability and Accountability Act defines the rights for medical patients, which includes medical coverage and information confidentiality

- Providing Appropriate Tools to Restrict, Intercept, and Obstruct Terrorism Act, known as the Patriot Act, covers a wide range of topics related to information sharing, verifying customer identification, and augmenting money laundering programs
- Trademark law is a unique symbol that distinguishes a company's product of services from that of other business entities

A number of laws passed by other countries also could impact the project. A few more recent laws that can impact international operations include:

- Personal Information Protection and Electronic Documents Act: A Canadian law protecting the data privacy of individuals in the commercial business environment
- European Union Data Protection Directive: Requires protecting the manual and automated processing of personal data
- Bribery Act of 2010: A British law that identifies financial and in-kind offers that are defined as criminal offenses during the solicitation of business
- Corruption of Foreign Public Officials Act: A Canadian law that prohibits the bribery of foreign government officials

In addition to laws, a number of frameworks, when implemented, minimize the potential occurrence of ethical risks that could confront an organization and its projects:

- Generally accepted accounting principles: A set of guidelines consisting of standards, procedures, and rules for financial accounting
- International financial reporting standards: A set of international principles forming a framework covering financial reporting
- Control objectives for information and related technology (COBIT): A governance framework to integrate technical and business controls to reduce the occurrence and impact of risks and issues
- Committee of Sponsoring Organizations (COSO): An integrated governance framework that enables companies to evaluate the effectiveness of their controls
- Organizational Project Management Maturity Model (OPM3®): A framework for developing and evaluating project, program, and portfolio management to determine and improve their performance; developed by the Project Management Institute

- Information Technology Library (ITIL™): A set of practices that enable effective delivery of information technology management services
- Capability maturity model integration (CMMI): A maturity model for assessing and improving the processes and practices of an information technology organization; developed by the Software Engineering Institute (SEI)

7.5 FINAL THOUGHTS

While compliance is just one consideration of many other topics concerning ethics, it is an important one because of the financial and legal consequences. Project managers need to determine to what extent their projects require legal compliance; failure to do so will put themselves and their organization at risk. Having a good knowledge of the governmental institutions, related nongovernmental organizations, methodologies, and legal terminology can help them respond to ethical issues and transgressions as they arise.

7.6 GETTING STARTED CHECKLIST

Question	Yes	No
1. Have you considered the following guidelines when looking at the relationship of ethics and the law as it applies to your project?		
Recognize that compliance includes more than the law		
Recognize that compliance is not passive; it is very active		
Understand that noncompliance requires taking corrective action		
Have a good understanding of any applicable laws but don't act as an attorney		
Realize that compliance does not stop unethical behavior; it simply minimizes the probability of occurrence		
Know that noncompliance can result from internal and external circumstances		

Question		Yes	No
	Be aware of the ethical laws applicable to your project and have a good understanding of the content and scope of those laws		
	Don't let current conduct and custom be your guide as a substitute for the compliance with the law		
	Don't gamble with obeying the law by calculating there is an acceptable loss or threshold in terms of fines because fines are only one part of the equation		
	Corporate social responsibility dictates that you and your project comply with the law		
2.	Have you considered whether some of the following U.S. organizations have some relationship to your project?		
	Bureau of Alcohol, Tobacco, Firearms, and Explosives		
	Bureau of Industry and Security		
	Commodity Credit Corporation		
	Council on Environmental Quality		
	Customs and Border Protection		
	Department of Commerce		
	Department of Treasury		
	Directorate of Defense Trade Controls		
	Equal Employment Opportunity Commission		
	Federal Financial institutions Examination Council		
	Food and Drug Administration		
	International Trade Association		
	National Labor Relations Board		
	Occupational Health and Safety Administration		
	Office of Federal Procurement Policy		
	Office of Government Standards		
	Overseas Private Investment Corporation		
	Securities and Exchange Commission		
	U.S. Customs Service		
	U.S. Export-Import Bank		

Continued

Question		Yes	No
	U.S. Federal Trade Commission		
	U.S. Trade Representative		
3.	Have you considered whether some of the following international organizations have some relationship to your project?		
	Asia-Pacific Economic Cooperation		
	Caux Round Table Business Principles of Ethics		
	Council of Europe Cybercrime Convention		
	European Union (EU)		
	General Agreement on Tariffs and Trade (GATT)		
	International Monetary Fund (IMF)		
	North American Free Trade Agreement (NAFTA)		
	Organization of Petroleum Exporting Countries (OPEC)		
	United Nations Conference on Trade and development (UNCTAD)		
	United nations Convention on Contracts for International Sale of Goods (CISG)		
	World Trade Organization (WTO)		
4.	Are you familiar with the following key legal terms and any others relevant to your project?		
	Acceptance		
	Agent		
	Arbitration		
	Bond		
	Breach		
	Condition		
	Conflict of interest		
	Consideration		
	Contract		
	Copyright		
	Damages		
	Defendant		
	Delegation of duties		

Question		Yes	No
	Delivery		
	Due process		
	Duty		
	Equity		
	Exoneration		
	Felony		
	Forbearance		
	Fraud		
	Good faith		
	Liability		
	Mediation		
	Misdemeanor		
	Misrepresentation		
	Negligence		
	Offer		
	Patent		
	Plaintiff		
	Precedent		
	Principal		
	Privity		
	Prosecutor		
	Remedy		
	Repudiation		
	Rescission		
	Right		
	Trademark		
	Waiver		
	Warranty		
5.	Are you aware of the following different categories of law?		
	Administrative		

Continued

Question		Yes	No
	Civil		
	Common		
	Criminal		
	Procedural		
	Statutory		
	Substantive		
6.	Are you keeping in mind the following principles and concepts as they relate to ethics and the law?		
	Recognize that all projects have a time of performance, meaning that projects start and finish within an agreed on time frame		
	Understand that laws involve some indication of an adequacy of performance, meaning the project management and products or services must meet certain minimum standards		
	Establish and maintain an audit trail of the work performed		
	Look for potential areas of fraud		
	Control access to critical or privileged information		
	Apply project management disciplines and techniques to the project as a demonstration of due diligence and due care		
	Provide oversight of suppliers and contractors related to your project		
	Be aware of the dangers associated with receiving gifts and other favors from vendors		
	Conduct a good risk assessment		
	Know the contract for your project		
	Understand that few, if any, projects operate in a legal "bubble," meaning that the tentacles of the law stretch far into most organizations today		
	Apply the proper exercise of authority		
	Comply with all internal and external audits and investigations		
	Apply effective controls on a project, especially if these relate to compliance		
	Don't become a "latrine lawyer"		
7.	Do any of the following laws from a general perspective apply to your project?		

Question		Yes	No
	Federal sentencing guidelines		
	Hobbs Act		
	International Emergency Economic Powers Act		
	Organized Crime Control Act		
	Uniform Commercial Code		
8.	Do any of the following environmental laws apply to your project?		
	Clean Air Act		
	Clean Water Act		
	Endangered Species Act		
	National Environmental Policy Act		
	Oil Pollution Act		
	Resource Conservation and Recovery Act		
	Safe Drinking Water Act?		
	Superfund Amendment & Reauthorization Act		
	Toxic Substances Control Act		
9.	Do any of the following financial laws apply to your project?		
	Anti-kickback Act		
	Bank Secrecy Act		
	Clayton Act		
	False Claims Act		
	Financial Services Modernization Act (also known as Gramm-Leach-Bliley Act		
	Money laundering Control Act		
	Robinson-Patman Act		
	Sarbanes-Oxley Act		
	Sherman Anti-Trust Act		
10.	Do any of the following labor laws apply to your project?		
	Age Discrimination in Employment Act		
	Americans with Disability Act		
	Civil Rights Act		

Continued

Question		Yes	No
	Employee Retirement Income Security Act		
	Equal Pay Act		
	Fair Labor Standards Act		
	Family and Medical Leave Act		
	Immigration and Nationality Act		
	Immigration Reform and Control Act		
	National labor Relations Act		
	Uniform Services Employment and Re-employment Rights Act		
11.	Do any of the following procurement laws apply to your project?		
	Federal Acquisition Regulations		
	Federal Acquisition Reform Act		
	Procurement Integrity Act		
	Truth in Negotiations Act		
12.	Do any of the following international trade laws apply to your project?		
	Arms Export Control Act		
	Customs Modernization Act		
	Export Administration Act		
	Export Administration Regulations		
	Export Control Acts		
	Export Trading Company Act		
	Foreign Corrupt Practices Act		
	International Traffic in Arms regulations		
	Webb-Pomerene Act		
13.	Do any of the following information technology and security laws apply to your project?		
	Computer Fraud and Abuse Act		
	Copyright Laws		
	Federal Information Security Management Act		
	Patent Laws		
	Privacy Act		
	Health Insurance Portability and Accountability Act		

Question		Yes	No
	Providing Appropriate Tools to Restrict, Intercept, and Obstruct Terrorism Act		
	Trademark laws		
14.	Do any of the following laws by other nations apply to your project?		
	Personal Information Protection and Electronic Documents Act		
	European Union Data Protection Directive		
	Bribery Act of 2010		
	Corruption of Foreign Publics Officials Act		
15.	Do any of the following frameworks apply to your project?		
	Generally accepted accounting principles		
	International financial reporting standards		
	Control objectives for information and related technology (COBIT)		
	Committee on Sponsoring Organizations (COSO)		
	Organizational Project Management Maturity Model (OPM3)		
	Information Technology Library (ITIL)		
	Capability maturity model integration (CMMI)		

8

Ethics, Globalization, and Project Management

The world of project management has changed in many respects. Projects are often no longer isolated events but rather a significant part of a company's success or failure, not just on a local level but an international level, too. Many projects now have a global dimension to them that also makes ethics a complicated concern for stakeholders on a project. Globalization in this context means that there is considerable integration among a wide number of people, processes, systems, and data that transcends national boundaries to generate a profit for a company.

8.1 IMPORTANT FACTORS

The relationship among project management, globalization, and ethics is complicated because of a number of factors:

- The competition has become more numerous, not just from other companies but from other countries.
- The time to market has accelerated. The company that delivers the earliest has the advantage of meeting customer needs and beating copycats.
- Quality has increased; many international companies adopt Six Sigma to deliver products and results that reduce rework and satisfy the needs of the customer.
- The development costs must drop to stay competitive, putting pressure to deliver at lower cost.
- On top of all that, pressure grows to increase shareholder value to ensure sufficient returns to investors.

Translated, all of this means that project managers must deliver faster, better, and cheaper. This pressure paves the way for ethical dilemmas in a global environment.

8.2 KEY DIMENSIONS

A project manager must consider several overlapping dimensions when working on international projects that can influence what is considered an ethical issue or transgression (Figure 8.1):

1. *Sociological dimension of international projects*: This dimension deals with topics like cultural aspects, such as religious holidays, beliefs and values, management and working styles, business and social protocols, perceptions of time, quality of life, risk and uncertainty, and perceptions of time and space.
2. *Political and legal dimension*: This pertains to the governing institutions of a society: This dimension deals with topics like law, regulations, political participation, and others principally centered on

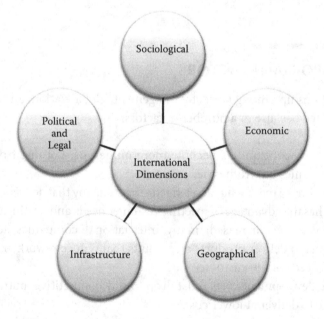

FIGURE 8.1
Ethical dimensions in the international environment.

the role of government; how it relates to internal constituencies and external parties; perceptions of ownership of enterprises and profits; government bureaucracy; and local acceptance of foreign powers.

3. *Economic dimension*: This pertains to topics like currency valuation, payments, supply and demand, perceptions about profit making and sharing, and foreign supplier relationships. Like the political dimension, this one is often dynamic, changing constantly.

4. *Infrastructure dimension*: This deals with technology, science, engineering, and others. This dimension deals with topics like the technological capacity of a country to support a project, standardization of tools and processes, information sharing, and technical proficiency and currency.

5. *Geographical dimension*: This requires considering the international, regional, and local factors when managing a project. Generally, the greater the geographical spread between the home for the project and the one for where the work is, the more difficult it is to manage, especially if the culture and technology varies from one location and the other. This dimension deals with topics like distance, time zones, and communication.

8.3 INDEPENDENCE, INTEGRATION, AND INTERDEPENDENCE

None of the dimensions should be seen as distinct among themselves; they are all interrelated to one degree or another. A change in one can impact another. And it can have ethical implications, too. For example, the politics can deteriorate between two countries, resulting in the two companies not interacting with each other. Each side can hold back information or sabotage the work of the others, causing a project to fail.

The relationships among all the aforementioned dimensions can become quite complex when the following three relationships are considered: independence, integration, and interdependence among all the elements of a project.

Independence reflects the degree of autonomy that each of the components (e.g., stakeholders, processes) has on a project. Interdependence is the degree of reliance the output of a component has on another component. Integration is the degree to which each component interacts with each other. In the global environment all three play a critical role in ensuring that all components work efficiently and effectively when delivering a product or service to the customer.

At first, it appears unclear why this is important from an ethical standpoint. The fact is that it is very important. If, for example, a key stakeholder, refuses to share information, deliberately does substandard work, or sells proprietary information to a competitor, then the entire relationship among the components can go awry, or get out of sync. In the global environment, this circumstance can have a high impact on the performance of a project where strategic, collaborative relationships are often common. If a partner or key supplier fails to perform, either by design or accident, the consequences can become quite apparent.

Culture, too, plays an important role in affecting the relationship among key stakeholders when it comes to ethical behavior. Culture, of course, is the totality of a host of factors like religion, ways of behaving, relationship protocols, and perception of time.

Kluckholn and Strodtbeck developed a framework to ascertain how different societies respond to different issues, concerns, or problems, which includes how people relate to their physical environment, seek immediate or delayed gratification, focus on a time spectrum consisting of the past, present, or future, perceive people in a negative or positive light, and prefer to work independently or collectively.* In a similar way, the Hofstede framework looks at four areas regarding culture: (1) individual or collective; (2) power; (3) uncertainty avoidance; and (4) masculinity versus femininity.† Thomas and Inkson identified three key elements for understanding what they refer to as cultural intelligence when it comes to ethics in a global environment: (1) knowledge of understanding a project manager's mental model for determining what is and is not ethical; (2) being mindful, identifying who will benefit and who will lose by a decision or action; and (3) behavioral skills, acknowledging that differences in values exist while at the same time adhering to a consistent, personal set of values.‡

Whether using these or other frameworks, they help in understanding how ethics are intertwined with culture. For example, using the Kluckholn and Strodtbeck framework, people from a culture that seeks to work independently may resist any teaming efforts to complete a major

---

* Clifford F. Gray and Erik W. Larson, *Project Management: The Managerial Process*, 4th ed. (Boston: McGraw-Hill Irwin, 2008), p. 498.
† Ibid., p. 499.
‡ David C. Thomas and Kerr Inkson, *Cultural Intelligence: People Skills for Global Business* (San Francisco: Berrett-Koehler, 2004), pp. 97–98.

deliverable for a project, regardless of impact to other stakeholders. People from an independent culture may deliberately decide to withhold key information or share other important resources for the overall good of a project because doing so may violate certain principles, such as political allegiance or historical animosity.

8.4 CHALLENGES

Ethics is not an easy topic to wrestle with in the international arena. Project managers must confront a number of challenges that can lead to ethical dilemmas and must deal with them.

There are the two fundamental perspectives of a team of people from different cultures: the host country and the home country. The perspectives can be quite dramatic, especially for someone who has not worked previously outside of their country. People become entrenched in their own culture and, if not given the appropriate time to adjust, can find it difficult to adapt. In other words, a person can experience culture shock, a real powerful inhibitor to the ability of some people to work with others. Over time, culture shock usually dissipates and the person adapts. If the culture is so engrained by the person from another country or the people of the host country then the relationships can deteriorate.

There is another fundamental question: Can good project performance be achieved while operating ethically? While most people answer yes, the answer does not become so clear when working on a crucial project that involves, for instant, a compressed schedule (e.g., fast-tracking). The pressure to deliver faster, better, and cheaper may result in people, either by design or accident, cutting corners using unethical means.

There are also differences in decision making. For example, some cultures take a long time to make a decision due to taking a collective approach; other cultures make decisions quickly due to one person using little deliberation. This challenge can frustrate either side if the circumstances cause considerable pressure to decide and act, resulting in one side ignoring the other.

Additionally, policies and procedures of two different firms can exist, especially those of companies from two different countries. The companies can operate like two battleships at sea that never quite sail in tandem because the crews of each one are doing something different on their vessels. In other words, all the cultural differences and the challenge get magnified because people operate under a different set of rules. This challenge is often more difficult for people working on the same team but not from the same company.

When projects involve people from one or more countries, many laws and regulations can also come into play. Stakeholders on a global project often have to be aware of the laws and regulations of not only their own country but also of those of other countries. These laws and regulations might have to do with immigration, taxation, environment, labor, or gift giving and may not be in sync.

Business protocols may also differ among multiple nationalities on a global project. Gift giving is a prime example where protocols vary widely. One company may have substantial restrictions placed on it by the home country while the host country does not; the exchange can then become very complicated when interpreting the law, leading easily to a potential ethical dilemma.

The infrastructure can add a challenge. This one includes roads, engineering, information technology, and the banking system of either the host or home country of the companies working together on a project. If one is less developed than the other, a company may find that it has no other choice but to take action that may circumvent the laws and regulations of a country to complete its work.

Also, motivation varies from one culture to the next. While all people share common physiological needs, the other needs, such as the ones identified by Abraham Maslow or Frederick Herzberg, begin to vary dramatically. In some cultures, the group rather than the individual becomes more important. In some other cultures, materialism continues to be of primary importance, whereas in others less tangible incentives seem to work. The differences can prove quite challenging on a project because if the expectations around motivation are not met then a breach of trust may arise, leading to a host of ethical dilemmas, often centered on not communicating.

How people process and act on information can vary, too. Some people from other cultures involve taking time to assess the information they receive and then act on it. Other people from different a culture may take little time to assess information then act upon it right away. Neither one is right or wrong, but, when the two vary, one may deliberately ignore the other, even to point of bringing a project to a standstill over differences in style rather than substance.

Value systems may also vary widely among individuals on a global project. In many respects this one is the hardest challenge and is often the source of legal complications, especially when it comes to gift giving and receiving or the treatment of certain team members. Project managers need to account for the differences in value systems because it affects the relationships among stakeholders and the quality of the results. They should also appreciate that laws and regulations often reflect cultural values and that failure to respect them can lead to ethical dilemmas.

Coupled with value systems, language is a major challenge and can lead to many inadvertent ethical dilemmas. Even if everyone on a project team speaks a common language like English, for example, the same word can have a different meaning to the person who spoke it and the one who heard it. Add values and geographical distance and the opportunity for problems is endless. Not just verbal language can be a problem. Body language can also pose a serious problem on a project. How people express themselves physically can influence how the message is interpreted, which means people react in a way that was never intended. Space, touch, and movement can all play a role in causing people to respond or react that can prove harmful to the outcome of a project.

Working styles can additionally lead to ethical complications. How people go about their responsibilities on the job differs, and such differences can become even more apparent between two or more people from unique cultures. Differences, for example, can occur over the breadth and depth of planning and following plans during execution. For some people, they may take shortcuts that may violate a policy or law to achieve a scheduled completion date.

Closely allied to the last point, management style can also contribute to ethical complications. Management style can vary from being extremely autocratic to being very laissez-faire. Too much of the former can cause people to hide ethical dilemmas for fear of being the messenger who is shot; in the latter, people take a view that ethics is a "nice to know" topic but is never to be taken seriously.

Working relationships, too, may produce ethical complications. Two different nationalities, which have a long historical animosity toward one another, can lead to some of their members on their project intentionally not saying anything to key people from the other nationality just for the sake of seeing the latter get into trouble despite having the responsibility to inform them.

Different attitudes toward risk taking can also vary from nationality to nationality. Some nationalities embrace change and are willing to take risks; others may be reluctant to take a risk. Either side may make a decision that can affect the outcome of a project. For example, some members of a team may be from a certain nationality that embraces risk taking; they decide to recklessly take an action without asking others about the consequences of a particular decision or action on the overall project or an entire organization.

Finally, social stratification within a particular culture can affect ethics on a project. Even people from the same nationality, especially traditionally hierarchical ones, may be overly obedient to their "superiors," laying the groundwork for subordinates to behave in ways that may violate the values of team members of another nationality.

Three additional factors pose challenges to projects in a global environment from an ethical perspective.

One, if the supply chain is immense and extremely integrated, communications and trust are important ingredients for success. Unfortunately, if at some point the level of communications and trust no longer works, the supply chain can break, after which time the potential for ethical issues and transgressions can occur (e.g., shipment of goods containing substandard components that could lead to injury or death to the consumer).

Two, trade barriers could become or are perceived as so onerous that importers and exporters try to circumvent them. This situation then entices them to seek illegal entry or egress from a country to meet cost and schedule constraints.

Third, historical animosities that seem to have dissipated over time can quickly reignite over differences in approach or even from the result of an international incident. Members of a project team may, for example, intentionally withhold information that could impact the performance of a project.

8.5 BREEDING GROUND AND CONSEQUENCES

The international environment provides a breeding ground for three unethical dilemmas that are frequently not found, or at least not as apparent, within the borders of the United States.

Cheaper labor and materials is the first. In the developing world, due mainly to historical circumstances, the world's supply of labor and non-labor resources is often considerably cheaper than those in developed countries. Developed countries may, and often do, exploit this situation by having projects that tap such inexpensive resources. This can lead to exploitation on projects that would likely never happen in the United States and most places in Europe. Ethics violation may include not respecting labor laws or exploiting children to develop deliverables for a project.

Countries with fewer laws and regulations is second. Some global companies will have international projects that have less government involvement, granting much flexibility in how they go about completing their projects. While there may not be an ethical violation from a legal perspective, they could still be performing ethical violations—nonetheless from a moral perspective. They could be using children, could be testing products on people before marketing deliverables in developed countries, or could be using political prisoners to do work for the project. International projects may also exploit countries having weaker environmental standards as well as virtually nonexistent labor laws.

Black market is the third. The black market is a subterranean economy that often reflects the free market more than the "official" one. People can buy goods and services that might not ordinarily be available to an open market of supply and demand. Some international projects may exploit the black market to obtain materials at costs and in quantities that may not be possible to acquire in the regular market at the desired level. In the black market, too, goods, not just money, can be exchanged. Operating in a black market is illegal in a country, of course, but the incentives from a monetary standpoint may be such that companies and their projects may engage in them.

Innumerable ethical issues may be of interest to companies and projects. Here is a just a sample list of topics relevant to a global project that may have potential ethical implications:

- Child labor
- Discrimination
- Employment hiring and dismissal
- Financial improprieties (e.g., money laundering)
- Forced labor (e.g., use of political prisoners)
- Gifts, bribery, and kickbacks

- Harassment (e.g., physical, sexual, psychological)
- Harmful products
- Human rights
- Immigration
- Intellectual property
- Marketing and advertising
- Pollution
- Price discrimination (e.g., price gouging, dumping)
- Privacy
- Sweatshops

Regardless of location, engaging in unethical activities on a global project can have severe consequences to the initiators of an unethical transgression and the recipients.

One consequence is the impact to the health, safety, and general welfare of the people, for example, who are being exploited or disrespected and the people who might be receiving the flawed final product or service.

Another consequence is the tarnished reputation of the parent company sponsoring the project that committed the unethical activity. With the rise of global communications via satellite television and the Internet, a major project that engages in unethical activities and gets discovered can ruin the reputation of a company almost overnight, causing its stock to plummet and the company to lose contracts.

Still another one is the fines and penalties that may be levied on a company and stakeholders on the applicable project. Even though the fines and penalties may be less than the gain from performing unethical business, it can impact any opportunity for a continued working relationship within the host country. In the end, the costs in terms of lost revenue and profits may far exceed the fines and penalties that the company could receive because of the unethical actions of people on a project.

8.6 KEY ACTIONS

International projects, therefore, can offer high rewards but if not handled in an ethical way can have a huge, negative impact on a company. If real or perceived unethical rewards are not handled correctly, then the negative consequences will become a reality. Project managers need to be aware of some of the actions to deal with unethical issues and transgressions that may arise.

One, team members should be encouraged to enhance cultural awareness. People should be urged to learn about the historical, customs, business protocols, politics, and other background information as a way to achieve higher levels of awareness. Such knowledge enables everyone to be more attuned to cultural sensitivities as well as to work with people from other cultures.

Two, identify the "normal" ways of doing business in a particular country. Every culture, even within different regions of a country, has unique protocols that it will be necessary to honor and respect. Of course, that does not mean doing something illegal; instead, it means understanding and reconciling what is permissible in all involved cultures. By no means should a project manager violate his country's or the host country's laws and regulation because that is the way of doing business. However, behaviors and actions should be honored that generate respect and honor among stakeholders.

Three, understand that cultural norms can vary within a country. The northern part of the country could be dramatically different in the conduct of business from other regions; what is permissible in one region, in other words, may not be permissible in other regions. This case exists especially in large countries with multiple ethnicities.

Four, remember that culture shock goes both ways. Whether a project is being managed in another country or in the United States, supervising a team of people from different countries adjustment can be quite difficult. There is a period of regret followed by acceptance of coming to another country. Anyone in such an environment is going to have a difficult time transitioning because their expectations and frame of reference need to adapt to the new environment. Failure to adapt may lead to inadvertently behaving in a certain way that may be construed as not only disrespectful but also unethical in the host country.

Five, seek to use a common language on an international project whether it is English, French, Spanish, or Mandarin. A common language, however, does not guarantee that everyone will communicate effectively and the team will perform like a well-oiled machine. That is because there may be differences in accents, in use of certain words, and interpretation of words. A simple word in English, for example, can have one connotation to one person and a totally different meaning to another, resulting in an unethical issue or transgression simply because the word was misinterpreted.

Six, be aware of the different frameworks for dealing with people from different cultures in a host country or in another. Many of these models center around what some people believe is a common set of values that are applicable no matter where a business relationship exists; these values, naturally, are applicable to projects, too.

- Tom Donaldson developed a framework that basically emphasizes that any negative responsibilities or duties avoid causing harm (referred to as minimalist) and that any positive ones provide positive support for a project (referred to as maximalist). He then identified 10 cross-cultural, universal values ranging from freedom of movement to right to a fair trial to free speech.[*]
- Richard DeGeorge also provides 10 guidelines related to ethics, including doing no intentional harm, respecting the rights of employees, respecting local culture, paying taxes, and cooperating with local governments.[†]
- Rushworth Kidder reduced the number of values for dealing ethically with people from other cultures. These values are even less tangible and include love, freedom, and fairness.[6]

A few international organizations or associations, such as Caux Round Table Business Principles of Ethics, have adopted some core principles for dealing with other cultures and countries across the globe. The principles cover topics like building a spirit of trust, having respect for the environment, treating employees with dignity and respect, and respecting human rights, to name just a few.[‡]

8.7 FINAL THOUGHTS

The key, of course, is subscribing not just to the concepts and principles herein but also to their actual exercise on a global project, whether within the United States or outside of it. Due diligence and due care are inseparable; both are

---

[*] Joseph Desjardins, *An Introduction to Business Ethics*, 2d ed. (Boston: McGraw-Hill, 2006), pp. 258–259.

[†] Ibid.

[‡] O. C. Ferrell, John Fraedrich, and Linda Ferrell, *Business Ethics: Ethical Decision Making and Cases*, 6th ed. (Boston: Houghton Mifflin Company, 2006), pp. 425–427.

necessary to ensure an ethical environment exists. A failure in due diligence will more likely lead to a failure in due care. A failure in due care is often a reflection of a failure of due diligence. Project managers, of course, should make a concerted effort to think and behave ethically and expect the same of other stakeholders regardless of whether a project is domestic or global. It is not enough to simply say, "When in Rome do what the Romans do."

8.9 GETTING STARTED CHECKLIST

Question		Yes	No
1.	If you have an international project, that is, one located in a host country or one consisting of people from different nationalities, did you look at it from the following dimensions?		
	Sociological		
	Political and legal		
	Economic		
	Infrastructure		
	Geographic		
2.	Did you consider using one of the many frameworks to understanding the cultural complexities behind your project, such as the following ones?		
	Kluckhorn and Strodtbeck[a]		
	Hostede[b]		
	Thomas and Inkson[c]		
3.	Have you considered some or all of the following challenges that you may face on your global project?		
	The host and home country perspectives		
	The ability to have good performance and operate ethically		
	Differences in decision making		
	Differences in policies and procedures		

[a] Clifford F. Gray and Eric W. Larson, Project Management: The Managerial Process, 4th ed. (Boston: McGraw-Hill Irwin, 2008), 498.
[b] Ibid., 499.
[c] David C. Thomas and Kerr Inkson. Cultural Intelligence: People Skills for Global Business (San Francisco: Berrett-Koehler, 2004), 97-98.

Continued

Question		Yes	No
	Varying laws and regulations		
	Different business protocols		
	Infrastructure capacity		
	Motivation		
	Difference in processing and acting upon information?		
	Differences in value systems		
	Language barriers		
	Differences in working style		
	Differences in management style		
	Working relationships		
	Different attitudes to risk taking		
	Social stratification		
	Supply chain complexity		
	Trade barriers		
	Nationalism		
4.	Does your global project operate in an environment that can lead to unethical behavior because of the following?		
	Cheap labor and materials		
	Countries with fewer laws and regulations		
	Resilient black market		
5.	If your project is in another country, do you have to be particularly mindful to avoid ethical issues and transgressions related to these and other topics?		
	Child labor		
	Discrimination		
	Employment hiring and dismissal		
	Financial improprieties, e.g., money laundering		
	Forced labor, such as use of political prisoners		
	Gifts, briberies, and kickbacks		
	Harassment, such as physical, sexual, psychological		
	Harmful products		
	Human rights		

Question		Yes	No
	Immigration		
	Intellectual property		
	Marketing and advertising		
	Pollution		
	Price discrimination, such as price gouging, dumping		
	Privacy		
	Sweatshops		
6.	If members on your global project are engaging in unethical conduct, have you considered the following consequence if you fail to stop it and it gets disclosed?		
	Impact to the health, safety, and general welfare of the people receiving the final product or service		
	The impaired reputation of you, your team members, and the entire company		
	Fines and penalties levied on you, others, and the company		
7.	If you face an unethical circumstance, have you considered taking some or all of the following actions?		
	Encourage you and your team members to enhance their cultural awareness		
	Identify normal ways of doing business in a particular country		
	Understand that cultural norms can vary within each country		
	Recognize that culture shock, for your countrymen and people from another country, goes both ways		
	Seek a common language		
	Be aware of different frameworks for dealing with people from different cultures in a host country or another		

9

Making Ethics a Reality

A common theme throughout this book is that project managers face many challenges when attempting to make ethics a major subject over their projects. Ethics just seems to take a backseat to topics like scheduling, estimating, building charters, applying earned value management, applying integrated change control, and many other concepts, tools, and techniques of project management. They can no longer accept this status quo if they have the desire to successfully resolve ethical dilemmas.

9.1 WHY ETHICS TAKES A BACK SEAT

There are many reasons ethics is not made a priority. It is frequently viewed as something people have to do because the higher-ups got the company in trouble and need to demonstrate to the shareholders and the government that they are doing something to make everyone ethical. The topic of ethics is considered by some to be touchy-feely and to enhance people's intellectual knowledge and nothing more. Someone with greater authority may think it is a good subject to talk it about but do not provide a work environment conducive to ethical behavior. It could also be viewed as a "flavor of the month" topic so common in corporate environments.

Ethics, particularly related to projects, is very serious. When ethics is used on projects, people can focus on performing their responsibilities rather than on deciding and acting in ways that can damage the reputation of the people on the project, the project itself, and the parent organization. In other words, people can concentrate on doing what is right and necessary to complete a project successfully. The negative aspects, of course, are that the people excessively take their time making decisions and actions, covering their tracks, and exploiting circumstances rather than focusing on performing their responsibilities in a way that leads to the successful execution of a project.

The best way to realize the importance of ethics is to compare projects with and without ethics. If project managers and other stakeholders think and act ethically, interim deliverables (e.g., a charter, plans, reports) will serve as reliable outputs that can be trusted to help produce the final deliverable to the customer. Everyone knows that the interim deliverables are the result of honest, trustworthy people and therefore can be used with a high degree of confidence. Now take a different perspective. If the project manager and other stakeholders are known to be unethical in thought and deed, to what extent will people have confidence in the interim deliverables and, ultimately, the final deliverable being produced? You guessed it: They will have very little faith in others and the output.

The lessons to bring from this scenario are twofold: Ethics has value on a project; and ethics has consequences. Ethics on a project is like blood. If unethical behavior is tolerated, then it will spread like tainted blood, damaging the organs. If ethical behavior is the norm, then it will allow the organs to do their jobs.

9.2 MAKING ETHICS ON PROJECTS A REALITY

Having good ethics on a project is not simple. Project managers must take action to allow good ethical decisions and behaviors to become the norm rather than the exception. Five actions will accomplish this:

One. embrace a code of ethics, regardless of professional organization. Most of them cover the same topics to varying degrees of breadth and depth. They provide standards and guidelines not only for routine situations but also for anomalous circumstances. Sometimes, people need a guidepost to help them navigate through difficult circumstances. The Project Management Institute (PMI) provides an excellent code of ethics that is applicable for all stakeholders to consider following on a project. It covers a wide range of topics, including responsibility, respect, fairness, conflict of interest, and honesty. Regardless of whether project managers are members of the PMI, they should all read its code of ethics. It is especially useful because it emphasizes taking a global perspective, serving as an excellent guide for dealing with ethical issues in an international environment.

Second, make ethics part of just about every significant decision or action, whether alone or as part of the group. Many decisions and actions have ethical consequences, some major and others minor. Asking and answering a simple question like, "Is this the right thing to do?" raises ethical considerations when making a decision or taking an action. An answer that is a categorical yes will likely not pose an ethical challenge to individuals. However, an answer that leaves some doubt should serve as a red flag, meaning that the decision or action requires some greater thought. If the decision or action makes people feel uneasy, there is some likelihood that a potentially ethical issue is involved.

Three, make ethics everyone's business. The idea that ethics is the concern of someone else is wrought with danger. Shifting responsibility can lead to people delegating, either vertically or horizontally in an organization, and can give people license to make unethical decisions and actions. In other words, it becomes someone else's concern. Everyone on the project team needs to take ownership of the ethical consequences of their decisions and actions.

Four, recognize that practicing ethics requires courage. Thinking, and even more so doing, the right thing is not easy. The pressures are immense in most corporate environments to conform. There are pressures from superiors, team members, colleagues, and other stakeholders to adhere to norms, mores, policies, and procedures. Any deviation, regardless of whether the decision or action is ethical, can result in being penalized, such as through ostracism, ridicule, and being ignored, demoted, and isolated. This courage, of course, is exhibited by all stakeholders, not just the project manager. Therefore, project managers need to provide an environment that tolerates and even encourages people to raise ethical concerns on a project. To do otherwise can sooner or later lead to unethical decisions and actions.

Five, remember that it is possible to have a successful completion of a project and still think and act ethically. Individuals can be ethical and still complete a project on time and within budget and satisfy customer goals and objectives. They are not diametrically opposed to each other. In fact, taking the high road in thought and deed will end up having positive consequences, even if the project finishes late, costs more than anticipated, and does not meet requirements; customers will likely make allowances for not succeeding because honesty and fairness has been practiced, for example, in working with them. Taking the low road, so to speak, will end up in an unsuccessful project even if the project finishes on time and within budget and meets requirements because the results of the unethical decisions and actions will surface later during the product life cycle such as through litigation, high maintenance costs, and tarnished reputation.

9.3 THE MARK OF AN ETHICAL PROJECT MANAGER

Exercising these five actions will help make ethics a major concern on projects if it is not already. Just as importantly, these steps encourage objective judgment on what is the right decision and response when dealing with ethical situations after considering all options, which is the mark of an ethical project manager.

9.4 GETTING STARTED CHECKLIST

	Question	Yes	No
1.	Does ethics take a backseat on your project? If so, is it because of the following?		
	Senior management members got in trouble and are enforcing ethics among the rank-and-file because of their ethical transgressions.		
	Stakeholders perceive ethics as a touchy-feely topic.		
	Someone higher up finds the topic interesting.		
	People perceive it as simply another "flavor of the month."		
2.	If you are trying to get stakeholders on your project to take ethics seriously on your project, have you done any of the following?		
	Embraced a code of ethics		
	Made ethics part of every significant decision or action		
	Made ethics everyone's business, not someone else's		
	Recognized that practicing ethics requires ethics		
	Remembered that it is possible to have a successful completion of a project and still think and act ethically		

Glossary

Acceptance: An agreement to accept a product or service being delivered

Accountability: Holding oneself responsible for results achieved

Accurate and timely information: The right information in the right amount and format at the right time

Administrative law: Laws passed for managing the affairs of government agencies

Agent: A person or organization acting on behalf of a customer or client

Arbitration: A binding decision by a third party

Aristotle: A Greek philosopher who wrote on a wide range of topics, including ethics

Bond: A promise to pay if there is a failure to perform

Breach: A failure, in whole or part, to perform according to contract

Bribe: The exchange of something of value, often money, to influence decisions or actions

Character: Traits or qualities that an individual or organization possesses that are exhibited when making decisions or taking action

Circumvention of quality standards: Knowingly allowing substandard workmanship by not adhering to standards

Civil law: A body of law established by nation states regarding the rights of its citizens

Closing: Concluding a project administratively and contractually

Code of ethics: Standards supported by guidelines to apply in the field

Commitment: Following through on what was promised

Common law: Legal rules setting precedents based on custom and their application by counts to make decisions

Compliance: Deals with adherence to, for example, policies, procedures, laws, and regulations

Condition: A requirement specified in a contract

Conflict of interest: A relationship that compromises the objectivity, independence, and loyalty to a business entity

Consideration: An exchange, either monetary or nonmonetary, such as an offset agreement for the development and delivery of a product or service

Control: A measure that you put in place that protects your project from threats or reduces its impact

Contract: A legal agreement that binds two or more parties to create a product or deliver a service

Copyright: An exclusive right to use original rights; requires permission from the original author to use

Corrective control: Taking action after a threat has occurred to rectify the situation and to ensure that circumstances get back to normal

Crashing: Concentrating resources on the critical path to improve schedule performance

Criminal law: A body of law dealing with crimes and punishment

Culture: The cumulative beliefs, values, norms, mores, processes, practices, stories, habits, etc. that occur in an environment

Cycle time: Regular, ongoing patterns of behavior that minimize deviation

Damages: Physical and nonphysical injuries a person or organization experiences due to a failure to perform

Defendant: The person or organization charged with committing a violation of law per the plaintiff

Delegation of duties: The transfer of obligations to another party without abdicating responsibility for results

Delivery: The product or service that is within the control of the customer

Deming wheel: Also known as the PDCA cycle and involves defining the objective, executing a plan, determining progress, and taking corrective action

Deontological ethics: Associated with one's particular behavior in regards to ethics based on universal truths or principles that identify what decisions and actions should and should not be taken

Detective control: A measure identifying the existence of a threat and is reported after its occurrence

Diogenes: A Greek philosopher famous for his philosophy of cynicism

Disinformation: False information spread intentionally

Due care: Taking all reasonable and necessary precautions to preclude harm

Due diligence: Establishing standards, procedures, and responsibilities to prevent illegal and unethical behavior

Due process: Laws protecting the rights of the individual vis-à-vis the government

Duty: The obligation to perform

Effectiveness: Addresses the achievement of goals and obligations

Efficiency: Deals with using resources in a manner that reduces waste

Employee health and safety: The work environment involving issues like ergonomics, carpel tunnel syndrome, and hazardous materials

Employee rights: Spans a wide breadth of topics including the right to privacy, use of equipment for personal means, and intellectual property

Employment at will: Deals with the contractual relationship between employees and their employers

Equity: The application of principles to compensate for the shortcomings and inequities of current laws and rules

Ethics: Exercising objective judgment after considering all options on what is the right decision and response when dealing with ethical situations

Ethical dilemma: Having to make a decision and action that goes down one path or the other

Ethnocentrism: The view that one's culture is superior to that of other cultures or nationalities

Executing: Carrying out the plans

Exoneration: An agreement not to hold a party liable for loss or failure to perform

Fairness: Being able to weigh the circumstances of an ethical situation when making a decision and taking action in a manner that is just for all parties

Fast tracking: Running many activities concurrently to accelerate schedule performance

Felony: A criminal act that results in incarceration for one or more years or is legislated as such

Forbearance: Prevented from performing an act, such as providing a service

Formal groups: The established formal groups within an organization, often shown in an organization chart

Fraud: A deliberate act to deceive by altering facts or making deliberate misstatements

Globalization: Enterprises, projects, and other organizations transcending national boundaries in terms of, for example, purpose or scope

Good faith: Lacking knowledge or awareness of any defect in the product or service delivered to the customer

Governance: Identifying and implementing the policies, processes, procedures, tools, and techniques for achieving specific goals and objectives

Hard technical topics: Those that can have legal and financial ramifications and are often quite apparent when a transgression occurs

Heuristic: A rule of thumb

Honesty: Expressing oneself in a way that encourages further dialogue and fact finding in contrast to being evasive or telling only part of a story

Independence: The degree of autonomy that each of the components has on a project

Informal groups: Groups not reflected in an organizational chart but having powerful influence

Integrity: The manifestation of character, that is, the cumulative beliefs and values of individuals

Initiating: The vision, mission, goals, objectives, and scope of the project in the form of a charter, statement of work, or contract or a combination of all three

Insider trading: Privileged information to which people within a corporation sometimes have access and that they use to their own advantage

Integration: The degree to which each component interacts with the other

Intellectual property: The application of, for example, exclusive rights to ideas or works that have an intangible quality

Intensity of response: The weight of a response

Interdependence: The degree of reliance the output of a component has on another component

Issue: Something that exists now and is no longer a risk

Jeremy Bentham: A utilitarian philosopher

John Stuart Mills: A utilitarian philosopher

Kickback: A form of bribe

Legal compliance: Adherence to laws and regulations

Liability: A civil wrong

Lowballing: Getting a contract with a customer by deliberately underbidding to get the contract and then jacking up costs once the contract has been signed

Management style: The overall managerial approach exhibited by leaders within an organization

Mediation: Nonbinding settlement of a dispute through a third party

Mischarging: Team members charging to the wrong charge line for their work or services

Misdemeanor: A violation of law that results in incarceration for less than 1 year or is not designated as a felony

Misrepresentation: A statement of fact falsely made without deception

Misinformation: Deliberate false information that is spread unintentionally

Misreporting: Massaging numbers or communicating them in such a way that trivializes their impact

Monitoring and controlling: Keeping abreast of how well the project is executing according to vision and plan

Morality: Consists of the customs, habits, mores, and values of a person or organization and is reflected in how decisions are made and action taken when dealing with ethical situations

Negligence: Not exercising appropriate action, resulting in harm to a person or organization

Offer: A person or organization expressing intent to enter into an agreement

Outsourcing: The exchange of payments or offsets for the services of external companies or other organizations

Padding: When estimates are artificially inflated for no other reason than to compensate for unknowns—not based on sound reasoning

Patent: Exclusive rights to an invention

PDCA cycle: Stands for Plan-Do-Check-Act; also known as the Deming Wheel

Plaintiff: The individual or organization filing a lawsuit against a defendant

Planning: Determining the roadmap for executing the contents of the charter, statement of work, or contract or a combination of all three

Plato: A Greek philosopher who focused, like his teacher Socrates, on ethics, logic, and mathematics

Power: The ability to influence means and outcomes on an institutional and personal level

Precedent: A court decision setting the standard for future legal decisions

Preventive control: Strategies put in place to offset or deter the occurrence of a threat

Principal: A person or organization that hires an agent to act on its behalf

Privity: A chain of relationships that must be followed

Procedural law: Rules followed by a court governing its activities

Prosecutor: The person who begins criminal proceedings against a defendant

Protection of resources: The physical and logical safekeeping of a project's resources

Red flag: A sign or signal indicating a cause for concern

Regulatory oversight: Regulating the affairs of business

Remedy: Activities to enforce payment of damages due to legal infringement

Repudiation: Refusal to perform one or more clauses of a contract

Rescission: One party decides to no longer follow a contract due to another party failing to execute according to the specified terms and conditions

Responsibility: Carrying out a commitment

Rewards: Incentives playing an instrumental role in affecting ethical decisions and behavior

Right: The capacity of a person or organization to require performance of an action by another party

Risk: A threat or opportunity

Risk assessment: Identifying and evaluating risks

Risk management: Identifying, evaluating, and responding to risks

Sensitivity of issue: The gravity of a situation or transgression

Socrates: A Greek philosopher who focused on ethics, logic, and epistemology

Soft ethical issues: Those that have financial and ethical consequences; often difficult to determine their occurrence and how to deal with them

Statutory law: Laws passed by legislative bodies

Structure: The organizational arrangement of components, such as people and other resources, often reflected in a hierarchy chart

Substantive law: Laws defining rights and responsibilities of individuals

Teleological ethics: Emphasizes the desired results to achieve, that is, placing importance on consequences when dealing with ethical situations

Threat: A vulnerability

Tone at the top: The general "atmosphere" or operating style established by executive management of an institution, such as a corporation

Trademark: A symbol identifying a product or service

Trust: Being able to depend on someone to exhibit consistent behavior that demonstrates honesty, straightforwardness, and reliability

Unfair competitive advantage: Information that gives a person or organization an advantage over competitors

Utilitarianism: A teleological philosophy that emphasizes consequences

Values: Beliefs exhibited when dealing with ethical situations but also when conducting normal business

Virtue: The traits or characteristics that make up the character of an individual or organization

Waiver: A release of an obligation

Warranty: A promise made in respect to the performance of a product

Bibliography

Arens, Alvin A. and Loebbecke, James K. *Auditing: An Integrated Approach*, 5th ed. Englewood Cliffs, NJ: Prentice Hall, 1991.

Axelrod, Alan. *My First Book of Business Ethics*. Philadelphia: Quirk Books, 2004.

Bennett, Bruce E., Bryant, Brenda K., VandenBos, Gary R., and Greenwood, Addison. *Professional Liability and Risk Management*. Washington, DC: American Psychological Association, 2004.

Berns, Gregory. *Iconoclast: A Neuroscientist Reveals How to Think Differently*. Boston: Harvard Business Press, 2008.

Biegelman, Martin T. and Bartow, Joel T. *Executive Roadmap to Fraud Prevention and Internal Control*. Hoboken, NJ: John Wiley & Sons, Inc., 2006.

Boatright, John R. *Ethics and the Conduct of Business*, 3rd ed. Upper Saddle River, NJ: Prentice Hall, 2000.

Callahan, David. *The Cheating Culture: Why More Americans Are Doing Wrong to Get Ahead*. Orlando, FL: Harcourt, Inc., 2004.

Ciulla, Joanne B. (Ed.). *Ethics: The Heart of Leadership*. Westport, CT: Praeger, 1998.

Cole, Eric and Ring, Sandra. *Insider Threat: Protecting the Enterprise from Sabotage, Spying, and Theft*. Rockland, MA: Syngress Publishing, Inc., 2006.

Colley, John L., Doyle, Jacqueline L., Stettinius, Wallace, and Logan, George. *Corporate Governance*. New York: McGraw-Hill, 2003.

Covey, Stephen M. R. *The Speed of Trust: The One Thing That Changes Everything*. New York: Free Press, 2006.

Covey, Stephen R. *Principle Centered Leadership*. New York: Fireside, 1992.

Czinkota, Michael R., Ronkainen, Ilkka A., and Rivoli, Pietra. *International Business*, 2nd ed. Fort Worth, TX: Dryden Press, 1992.

Daniels, John D. and Radebaugh, Lee H. *International Business: Environments and Operations*, 9th ed. Upper Saddle River, NJ: Prentice Hall, 1998.

DesJardins, Joseph. *An Introduction to Business Ethics*, 2nd ed. Boston: McGraw-Hill, 2006.

Ferrell, O. C., Fraedrich, John, and Ferrell, Linda. *Business Ethics: Ethical Decision Making and Cases*, 6th ed. Boston: Houghton Mifflin Company, 2006.

Gray, Clifford F. and Larson, Erik W. *Project Management: The Managerial Process*, 4th ed. Boston: McGraw-Hill Irwin, 2008.

Halberstam, Joshua. *Everyday Ethics*. New York: Viking, 1993.

Hall, Vanessa. *The Truth About Trust in Business*. Austin, TX: Emerald Book Club, 2009.

Jackall, Robert. *Moral Mazes: The World of Corporate Managers*. New York: Oxford University Press, 1988.

Jennings, Marianne M. *Business Ethics: Case Studies and Selected Readings*, 5th ed. Australia: Thomson South-Western, 2006.

Johnson, Craig E. *Ethics in the Workplace: Tools and Tactics for Organizational Transformation*. Thousand Oaks, CA: Sage Publications, 2007.

Maxwell, John C. *There's No Such Thing as "Business" Ethics: There's Only One Rule for Making Decisions*. New York: Warner Business Books, 2003.

McCann, David. And Not a Moment Too Soon. *CFO*. January 2008.

Mulcahy, Rita. *PMP Exam Prep, 6th ed.* Minnetonka, MN: RMC Publications, 2009.

PM Network. Hot July Button. July 2007.

PM Network. In Trouble. September 2006.

PM Network. The Leadership Track. October 2010.

PM Network. We're All Doomed Unless You Start Talking. June 2007.

Reina, Dennis S. and Reina, Michelle L. *Trust and Betrayal in the Workplace: Building Effective Relationships in Your Organization.* San Francisco: Berrett-Koehler Publishers, Inc., 2006.

Schinzinger, Roland and Martin, Mike W. *Introduction to Engineering Ethics.* Boston: McGraw-Hill, 2000.

Terkel, Susan N. *Ethics.* Dutton: Lodestar Books, 1992.

Thomas, David C. and Inkson, Kerr. *Cultural Intelligence: People Skills for Global Business.* San Francisco: Berrett-Koehler Publishers, Inc., 2004.

Twoney, David P. and Jennings, Marianne M. *Law and Business: Revised Edition for Bellevue Community College.* Australia: Cengage Learning, 2008.

Welytok, Jill G. *Sarbanes-Oxley for Dummies,* 2nd ed. Hoboken, NJ: John Wiley & Sons, Inc., 2008.

White, Thomas I. *Business Ethics: A Philosophical Reader.* Upper Saddle River, NJ: Prentice Hall, 1993.

Index

A

Accountability, 29, 113
  diffusion of, 80–81
Accuracy of information, in project
  governance, 153
Administrative law, 168, 207
Advertising, 196
Age Discrimination in Employment Act,
  174
Agencies, 165–166
Agreement, desire for, 94–95
Americans with Disability Act, 174
Anti-kickback Act, 174
Arbitrary employment, 26
Arbitration, 167, 207
Arms Export Control Act, 175
Asia-Pacific Economic Cooperation, 166
Associations, membership, 52
Assumptions, 37–38
Authority, obedience to, 81–82
Authorization, 116

B

Bad, good, determining difference, 2
Bank Secrecy Act, 174
Behavior reflecting beliefs, 29
Beliefs, behavior reflecting, 29
Beliefs/behavior, congruence between,
  73–74
Benefits of code of ethics, 47–48
Black market, 195
Bond, 167, 207
Breach of contracts, 26, 207
Bribery, 195
Bribery Act of 2010, 177
Bribes, 26, 207
Bureau of Alcohol, Tobacco, Firearms,
  and Explosives, 165
Bureau of Industry and Security, 165

C

Capability maturity model integration,
  178
Career, 50–52
Caretaking, 50, 54–55
Caring, 50, 58–61
Caux round table business principles of
  ethics, 166, 180, 198
Character, 13–14, 50–51, 207
Child labor, 195
CISG. See United Nations Convention on
  Contracts for International Sale
  of Goods
Civil law, 168, 207
Civil Rights Act, 174
Clayton Act, 174
Clean Air Act, 173
Clean Water Act, 173
Closing project, 103–104, 127–129, 207
Cloudy perspective, 32–33
CMMI. See Capability maturity model
  integration
COBIT. See Control objectives for
  information and related
  technology
Code of ethics, 47–68
  benefits of, 47–48
  contents, 50
  principles, categories of, 49–64
  professional societies, 52
Coercion, 133
Collaboration, 120
Commitment, 29, 50, 62–63, 207
Committee of Sponsoring Organizations,
  177
Commodity Credit Corporation, 165
Common controls in project governance,
  sample of, 154–155
Common law, 168, 207
Communication, 31, 50, 57–58

Company reputation, 146
Competency, 50, 52–54
Competing priorities, 30–31
Competition, 8
Compliance, 5, 50, 63–64, 72, 104, 207
  legal, emphasis on, 82–83
  in project governance, 153
Computer Fraud and Abuse Act, 176
Conduct, 50, 61–62
Confidentiality, 50, 56, 116
Conflict of interest, 26, 84–85, 167, 207
Conflicting laws, regulations, 83–84
Confronting problems, 144
Consequences of ethical failure, 31–32
Consideration, 167, 207
Contents, 50
Contextual factors, 101–102
Contracts, 167, 208
  breach of, 26
Control objectives for information and
    related technology, 177
Controlling project, 103, 122–127
Controls, in project governance, defined,
    153
Copying, unauthorized, 121–122
Copyright, 167, 208
  Copyright Law, 176
Corrective action, 73
Corruption of Foreign Public Officials
    Act, 177
COSO. See Committee of Sponsoring
    Organizations
Cost of materials, 195
Council of Europe cybercrime convention,
    166
Council on Environmental Quality, 165
Credibility, 31, 73
Criminal law, 168, 208
Culture, 7
Customer satisfaction, 88–89
Customs and Border Protection, 165
Customs Modernization Act, 175
Customs Service, U.S., 166
Cycle time, 87–88

D

Damages, 167, 208
Data to generate information, 124–125

Deception, 144–145
Defective products, 121
Defendants, 167, 208
Defining ethics, 1–3
Delegation of duties, 167, 208
Deontological ethics, 16, 208
Department of Commerce, 165
Department of Treasury, 165
Desire for agreement, 94–95
Dilemmas, ethical, 33–35, 72–73,
    129–146
Diligence, 25
Directorate of Defense Trade Controls,
    165
Discrimination, 136, 195
Disinformation, 114–116
Dismissal, 195
Dismissing, 120–121
Dissent, 119
Due care, 25, 72, 140–141
Due diligence, 25, 72, 140–141
Due process, 167, 208
Dumping, 196
Dysfunctional motivation, 30

E

Effectiveness, 105
  in project governance, 153
Efficiency, 106
  effectiveness, trade-offs, 78–79
  in project governance, 153
Employee Retirement Income Security
    Act, 174
Employee rights, 26, 177
Employment, arbitrary, 26
Endangered Species Act, 173
Enforcement of standards, 122
Environmental laws, regulations, 173
Equal Employment Opportunity
    Commission, 165
Equal Pay Act, 174
Equitable treatment, 137
Equity, 167, 209
Ethical dilemmas, 33–35, 72–73, 129–146
Ethical situations, 2
EU. See European Union
European Union, 166
  Data Protection Directive, 177

Executing project, 103, 114–122
Exoneration, 167, 209
Expectations
    clarifying, 109–110
    meeting, 85–86
Expense reports, inflating, 126
Expertise, 52
Exploitation, 138
Export Administration Act, 176
Export Administration Regulations, 176
Export Control Acts, 176
Export-Import Bank, 166
Export Trading Company Act, 176
Extreme behavior, 29

F

Failure, ethical
    consequences of, 31–32
    legal consequences, 31–32
Fair labor Standards Act, 175
Fairness, 14–15
False Claims Act, 174
Falsifying records, 129
Family and Medical Leave Act, 175
Federal Acquisition Reform Act, 175
Federal acquisition regulations, 175
Federal Financial Institutions
        Examination Council, 165
Federal Information Security
        Management Act, 176
Federal sentencing guidelines, 172
Federal Trade Commission, 166
Feedback, 134, 141–142
Financial laws, regulations, 173–174
Food and Drug Administration, 165
Forced labor, 195
Foreign Corrupt Practices Act, 176
Frameworks, 177–178
Fraud, 167, 209

G

GATT. *See* General Agreement on Tariffs
        and Trade
General Agreement on Tariffs and Trade,
        166
Generally Accepted Accounting
        Principles, 177

Gifts, inappropriate, 139–140
Global trends, 69–71
    access to information, 86–87
    accountability, diffusion of, 80–81
    adapting to, 71–74
    agreement, desire for, 94–95
    beliefs/behavior, congruence between,
        73–74
    compliance, 72
    conflict of interest, 84–85
    conflicting laws, regulations, 83–84
    corrective action, 73
    credibility, 73
    customer satisfaction, 88–89
    cycle time, 87–88
    due care, 72
    due diligence, 72
    efficiency/effectiveness, trade-offs,
        78–79
    ethical dilemmas, 72–73
    expectations, meeting, 85–86
    globalization, 69
    intellectual property, 69–70
    legal compliance, emphasis on, 82–83
    numbers, reliance on, 93
    obedience to authority, 81–82
    outsourcing, 70–71
    PDCA cycle, 73
    positive data, pressure to report, 76–77
    positive working relationships, 95–96
    regulatory oversight, 70
    speed of results, 77–78
    strategic priority, 71–72
    team players, 89–90
    technology, reliance on, 71
    transglobal operations, 79–80
    trustee perspective, 72
    workplace rights, 70
Globalization, 69, 187–201
    actions, 196–198
    advertising, 196
    black market, 195
    bribery, 195
    challenges, 191–194
    child labor, 195
    dimensions, 188–189
    discrimination, 195
    dismissal, 195
    economic dimension, 189

ethical dimensions, 188
factors, 187–188
financial improprieties, 195
forced labor, 195
geographical dimension, 189
harassment, 196
harmful products, 196
hiring, 195
human rights, 196
immigration, 196
independence, 189–191
infrastructure dimension, 189
intellectual property, 196
kickbacks, 195
labor, cost of, 195
legal dimension, 188–189
marketing, 196
materials, cost of, 195
political dimension, 188–189
pollution, 196
price discrimination, 196
privacy, 196
sociological dimensions, 188
sweatshops, 196
Good, bad, determining difference, 2
Good faith, 167, 209
negotiations, 111
Governance of project, 151–162
accurate information, 153
common controls, sample of, 154–155
compliance, 153
controls, defined, 153
defining governance, 151–152
effectiveness, 153
efficiency, 153
resource protection, 153
risk
defined, 153–155
management of, 156–158
timely information, 153
Gramm-Leach-Bliley Act, also known
as Financial Services
Modernization Act, 174

H

Harassment, 132, 196
Hard ethical issues, 24–31
Harmful products, 196

Health Insurance Portability and
Accountability Act, 176
Hidden agendas, 137–138
Hobbs Act, 173
Honesty, 12
Human rights, 196

I

Illicit activities, 142
IMF. *See* International monetary fund
Immigration, 196
Immigration and Nationality Act, 175
Immigration Reform and Control Act, 175
Importance of ethics, 21–45
accountability, 29
arbitrary employment, 26
assumptions, 37–38
behavior reflecting beliefs, 29
breach of contracts, 26
bribes, 26
cloudy perspective, 32–33
commitment, 29
competing priorities, 30–31
conflicts of interest, 26
consequences of ethical failure, 31–32
credibility, 31
dilemmas, 34
due care, 25
due diligence, 25
dysfunctional motivation, 30
employee rights, 26
ethical dilemmas, 33–35
extreme behavior, 29
hard ethical issues, 24–31
impact of response, 38
inaccurate reporting, 28
insider trading, 27
intensity-sensitivity matrix, 35
issues involving ethics, 25
judgment continuum, 38
kickbacks, 26
legal consequences of ethical failure,
31–32
legal noncompliance, 25
long-term perspectives, unbalanced,
28–29
low-balling, 27
mischarging, 27

padding, 27
performance pressure, 30
poor communication, 31
repressive culture, 29
reputation, 31
responsibility, 29
soft ethical issues, 24–31
stakeholder impact, 37
substandard quality, 27–28
unbalanced short-term perspectives,
      28–29
unfair competitive advantage, 28
unique circumstances, 21–24
Inaccurate reporting, 28
Incivility, 131
Infighting, 136–137
Information, 105
   access to, 86–87
Information technology, security laws,
      176–177
Information Technology Library, 178
Initiating project, 103, 107
Insider trading, 27, 210
Integrity, 15
Intellectual property, 69–70, 196
Intensity-sensitivity matrix, 35
International Emergency Economic
      Powers Act, 173
International financial reporting
      standards, 177
International guidelines, 166
International Monetary Fund, 166
International operations, 177
International Trade Administration, 165
International trade laws, regulations,
      175–176
International Traffic in Arms Regulations,
      176
ITIL. *See* Information Technology Library

J

Judgment, 2
   continuum of, 38

K

Kickbacks, 26, 195, 207
Knowledge, 52

L

Labor
   cost of, 195
   laws, regulations, 174–175
Law, ethics, relationship, 163–166
Legal compliance, emphasis on, 82–83
Legal consequences of ethical failure,
      31–32
Legal issues, 163–185
   administrative law, 168
   Age Discrimination in Employment
      Act, 174
   agencies, 165–166
   Americans with Disability Act, 174
   Anti-kickback Act, 174
   Arms Export Control Act, 175
   Asia-Pacific Economic Cooperation,
      166
   Bank Secrecy Act, 174
   Bribery Act of 2010, 177
   Bureau of Alcohol, Tobacco, Firearms,
      and Explosives, 165
   Bureau of Industry and Security, 165
   Capability maturity model integration,
      178
   Caux round table business principles
      of ethics, 166, 180, 198
   civil law, 168
   Civil Rights Act, 174
   Clayton Act, 174
   Clean Air Act, 173
   Clean Water Act, 173
   Committee of Sponsoring
      Organizations, 177
   Commodity Credit Corporation, 165
   common law, 168
   Computer Fraud and Abuse Act, 176
   Control objectives for information and
      related technology, 177
   Copyright Law, 176
   Corruption of Foreign Public Officials
      Act, 177
   Council of Europe cybercrime
      convention, 166
   Council on Environmental Quality,
      165
   criminal law, 168
   Customs and Border Protection, 165

Customs Modernization Act, 175
Department of Commerce, 165
Department of Treasury, 165
Directorate of Defense Trade Controls, 165
Employee Retirement Income Security Act, 174
Endangered Species Act, 173
environmental laws, regulations, 173
Equal Employment Opportunity Commission, 165
Equal Pay Act, 174
European Union, 166
European Union Data Protection Directive, 177
Export Administration Act, 176
Export Administration Regulations, 176
Export Control Acts, 176
Export Trading Company Act, 176
Fair labor Standards Act, 175
False Claims Act, 174
Family and Medical Leave Act, 175
Federal Acquisition Reform Act, 175
Federal acquisition regulations, 175
Federal Financial Institutions Examination Council, 165
Federal Information Security Management Act, 176
Federal sentencing guidelines, 172
financial laws, regulations, 173–174
Food and Drug Administration, 165
Foreign Corrupt Practices Act, 176
frameworks, 177–178
General Agreement on Tariffs and Trade, 166
general laws, regulations, 172–173
Generally Accepted Accounting Principles, 177
Gramm-Leach-Bliley Act, also known as Financial Services Modernization Act, 174
Health Insurance Portability and Accountability Act, 176
Hobbs Act, 173
Immigration and Nationality Act, 175
Immigration Reform and Control Act, 175
information technology, security laws, 176–177

Information Technology Library, 178
International Emergency Economic Powers Act, 173
International financial reporting standards, 177
international guidelines, 166
International Monetary Fund, 166
international operations, 177
International Trade Administration, 165
international trade laws, regulations, 175–176
International Traffic in Arms Regulations, 176
labor laws, regulations, 174–175
law, ethics, relationship, 163–166
laws, 172–178
legal principles, 168–172
Money Laundering Control Act, 174
National Environmental Policy Act, 173
National Labor Relations Act, 175
National Labor Relations Board, 165
North American Free Trade Agreement, 166
Occupational Health and Safety Administration, 165
Office of Federal Procurement Policy, 165
Office of Government Standards, 165
Oil Pollution Act, 173
Organization of Petroleum Exporting Countries, 166
Organizational Project Management Maturity Model, 177
Organized Crime Control Act, 173
Overseas Private Investment Corporation, 165
Patent Law, 176
Personal Information Protection and Electronic Documents Act, 177
Privacy Act, 176
procedural law, 169
Procurement Integrity Act, 175
procurement laws, regulations, 175
Providing Appropriate Tools to Restrict, Intercept, and Obstruct Terrorism Act, 177

Racketeer Influenced and Corrupt
 Organizations, 173
regulations, 172–178
Resource Conservation and Recovery
 Act, 173
Robinson-Patman Act, 174
Safe Drinking Water Act, 173
Sarbanes-Oxley Act, 174
Securities and Exchange Commission,
 166
Sherman Anti-Trust Act, 174
statutory law, 169
substantive law, 169
Superfund Amendment and
 Reauthorization Act, 173
Toxic Substances Control Act, 173
Trademark law, 177
Truth in Negotiations Act, 175
Uniform Commercial Code, 173
Uniform Services Employment and
 Re-employment Rights Act,
 175
United Nations Conference on Trade
 and Development, 166
United Nations Convention on
 Contracts for International Sale
 of Goods, 166
U.S. Customs Service, 166
U.S. Export-Import Bank, 166
U.S. Federal Trade Commission, 166
U.S. Trade Representative, 166
Webb-Pomerene Act, 176
World Trade Organization, 166
Legal noncompliance, 25
Life cycle of project, 101–150
 access to information, 142
 accountability, 113
 authorization, 116
 bad news, reporting, 125–126
 closing project, 103–104, 127–129
 coercion, 133
 collaboration, 120
 company reputation, 146
 compliance, 104
 confidentiality, 116
 conflicting interest, 109
 confronting problems, 144
 contextual factors, 101–102
 controlling project, 103, 122–127

 copying, unauthorized, 121–122
 data to generate information, 124–125
 deception, 144–145
 defective products, 121
 delivering results, 128
 discrimination, 136
 disinformation, 114–116
 dismissing, 120–121
 dissent, 119
 due care, 140–141
 due diligence, 140–141
 effectiveness, 105
 efficiency, 106
 employee rights, 177
 enforcement of standards, 122
 equitable treatment, 137
 ethical dilemmas, 129–146
 executing project, 103, 114–122
 expectations, clarifying, 109–110
 expense reports, inflating, 126
 exploitation, 138
 falsifying records, 129
 feedback, 134, 141–142
 gifts, inappropriate, 139–140
 good faith negotiations, 111
 harassment, 132
 hidden agendas, 137–138
 illicit activities, 142
 incivility, 131
 infighting, 136–137
 information, 105
 initiating project, 103, 107
 low-balling, 107–108
 lying, 110, 113
 mischarging, 114
 misinformation, 114–116
 misreporting, 122–124
 monitoring project, 103, 122–127
 organizational goals, misaligning with,
  108–109
 padding, 111–113
 peers, respect for, 117–118
 perception, 144–146
 performance, 143–144
 personal responsibility, 134–135
 planning project, 103, 111–113
 plans to report progress, 125
 power, 135–136
 privacy, 132

privileged information, 143–144
processes, 103–104, 106–111
reporting bad news, 125–126
reporting unethical behavior, 143
reputations, 138–139
resources, protection of, 106
retaliation, 132–133
rumors, 135
satisfying contractual requirements,
   128–129
stakeholders
   omitting, 108
   sabotaging relationships with,
     110–111
   sharing information with, 124
suppliers, conflict of interest, 140
team members, 119
   treatment of, 120
temporary relationships, 102
time pressure, 102
toxic culture, 131
treatment of people, 134
underperforming, 118
values, respect for, 133–134
vendors, conflict of interest, 140
vital information, destroying, 126–127
working relationships, 116–117
Long-term perspectives, unbalanced,
   28–29
Low-balling, 27, 107–108, 211
Lying, 110, 113

M

Management style, 10
Marketing, 196
Materials, cost of, 195
Mediation, 168, 210
Mischarging, 27, 114
Misdemeanor, 168, 210
Misinformation, 114–116
Misperceptions about ethics, 3–6
Misreporting, 122–124
Misrepresentation, 168, 210
Money laundering, 195
   Money Laundering Control Act, 174
Monitoring project, 103, 122–127
Morality, 12–13
Motivation, dysfunctional, 30

N

NAFTA. *See* North American Free Trade
   Agreement
National Environmental Policy Act, 173
National Labor Relations Act, 175
National Labor Relations Board, 165
Negligence, 168, 211
Noncompliance, legal, 25
North American Free Trade Agreement,
   166
Numbers, reliance on, 93

O

Obedience to authority, 81–82
Occupational Health and Safety
   Administration, 165
Offers, 168, 211
Office of Federal Procurement Policy, 165
Office of Government Standards, 165
Oil Pollution Act, 173
OPEC. *See* Organization of Petroleum
   Exporting Countries
OPM3. *See* Organizational Project
   Management Maturity Model
Organization of Petroleum Exporting
   Countries, 166
Organizational goals, misaligning with,
   108–109
Organizational Project Management
   Maturity Model, 177
Organized Crime Control Act, 173
Outsourcing, 70–71
Overseas Private Investment Corporation,
   165

P

Padding, 27, 111–113, 211
Partners, relationship with, 95–96
Patents, 168, 211
   Patent Law, 176
PDCA cycle, 73
Peers, 6–7
   respect for, 117–118
Perception, 144–146
Performance, 143–144
   pressure, 30

Personal Information Protection and Electronic Documents Act, 177
Personal responsibility, 134–135
Physical harassment, 196
Plaintiffs, 168, 211
Planning project, 103, 111–113
Plans to report progress, 125
Pollution, 196
Positive data, pressure to report, 76–77
Positive working relationships, 95–96
Power, 7–8, 135–136
Precedent, 168, 211
Pressure to report positive data, 76–77
Price
  discrimination, 196
  gouging, 196
Principals, 168, 211
Priorities, competing, 30–31
Prisoners, political, use of, 195
Privacy, 132, 196
  Privacy Act, 176
Privileged information, 143–144
Privity, 168, 211
Procedural law, 169, 211
Procurement Integrity Act, 175
Procurement laws, regulations, 175
Professional societies, 52
Project governance, 151–162
Project manager, 206
Prosecutor, 168, 211
Providing Appropriate Tools to Restrict, Intercept, and Obstruct Terrorism Act, 177
Psychological harassment, 196

R

Racketeer Influenced and Corrupt Organizations, 173
Regulations, 172–178
  conflicting, 83–84
Regulatory oversight, 70
Reliance on numbers, 93
Remedies, 168, 211
Reporting
  bad news, 125–126
  inaccurate, 28
  unethical behavior, 143
Repressive culture, 29

Repudiation, 168, 211
Reputation, 31, 138–139
Rescission, 168, 211
Resource Conservation and Recovery Act, 173
Resources, protection, 106
  in project governance, 153
Responses
  impact of, 38
  to situations, determining, 2–3
Responsibility, 29
Results, speed of, 77–78
Retaliation, 132–133
Rewards, 8–9
RICO. *See* Racketeer Influenced and Corrupt Organizations
Rights, 168, 212
Risk management in project governance, 156–158
Risks in project governance, defined, 153–155
Robinson-Patman Act, 174
Role expectations, 9
RTO. *See* World Trade Organization
Rumors, 135

S

Safe Drinking Water Act, 173
Sarbanes-Oxley Act, 174
Satisfying contractual requirements, 128–129
Securities and Exchange Commission, 166
Sexual harassment, 196
Sherman Anti-Trust Act, 174
Short-term perspectives, 28–29
Situations, determining responses to, 2–3
Sociological dimensions, 188
Soft ethical issues, 24–31, 212
Speed of results, 77–78
Stakeholders
  impact on, 37
  omitting, 108
  relationship with, 95–96
  sabotaging relationships with, 110–111
  sharing information with, 124
Status, protecting, 96–97
Statutory law, 169, 212
Strategic priority, 71–72

Substandard quality, 27–28
Substantive law, 169, 212
Superfund Amendment and
        Reauthorization Act, 173
Suppliers, conflict of interest, 140
Sweatshops, 196

T

Teams, 119
    members of, 89–90
    treatment of, 120
Technology, reliance on, 71
Teleological ethics, 16, 212
Temporary relationships, 102
Terminology, 10–15
Theoretical underpinnings, 15–17
    deontological ethics, 16
    teleological ethics, 16
Time pressure, 102
Timely information in project governance,
    153
Toxic culture, 131
Toxic Substances Control Act, 173
Trade Representative, U.S., 166
Trademarks, 168, 212
    Trademark law, 177
Transglobal operations, 79–80
Trust, 12
Trustee perspective, 72
Truth in Negotiations Act, 175

U

UCC. *See* Uniform Commercial Code
Unbalanced short-term perspectives, 28–29
UNCTAD. *See* United Nations Conference
    on Trade and Development

Underperforming, 118
Unfair competitive advantage, 28, 212
Uniform Commercial Code, 173
Uniform Services Employment and
        Re-employment Rights Act, 175
Unique circumstances, 21–24
United Nations Conference on Trade and
        Development, 166
United Nations Convention on Contracts
        for International Sale of Goods,
        166
U.S. Customs Service, 166
U.S. Export-Import Bank, 166
U.S. Federal Trade Commission, 166
U.S. Trade Representative, 166

V

Values, 11
    respect for, 133–134
Vendors
    conflict of interest, 140
    relationship with, 95–96
Virtue, 14
Vital information, destroying, 126–127

W

Waiver, 168, 212
Warranty, 168, 212
Webb-Pomerene Act, 176
Working relationships, 95–96, 116–117
Workplace rights, 70
World Trade Organization, 166

Y

Yiddish, terminology usage, 48

Printed in the United States
by Baker & Taylor Publisher Services